ORDINARY WARS

Doing Transdisciplinary Research

Genevieve Durham DeCesaro
Elizabeth A. Sharp

ORDINARY WARS

Doing Transdisciplinary Research

Genevieve Durham DeCesaro
Elizabeth A. Sharp

Common Ground Publishing 2016

First published in 2016 in Champaign, Illinois, USA
by Common Ground Publishing LLC
as part of The Arts in Society book imprint

Copyright © Genevieve Durham DeCesaro and Elizabeth Sharp 2016

All rights reserved. Apart from fair dealing for the purposes of study, research, criticism or review as permitted under the applicable copyright legislation, no part of this book may be reproduced by any process without written permission from the publisher.

Library of Congress Cataloging-in-Publication Data

Names: Durham DeCesaro, Genevieve, author. | Sharp, Elizabeth (Elizabeth A.), author.
Title: Ordinary wars : doing transdisciplinary research / Genevieve Durham DeCesaro, Elizabeth Sharp.
Description: Champaign, Illinois : Common Ground Publishing, 2016. | Includes bibliographical references and index.
Identifiers: LCCN 2015048876 (print) | LCCN 2016010898 (ebook) | ISBN 9781612298429 (pbk : alk. paper) | ISBN 9781612298436 (pdf) | ISBN 9781612298429 (pbk)
Subjects: LCSH: Social sciences--Research--Methodology. | Interdisciplinary research. | Dance--Social aspects.
Classification: LCC H62 .D8155 2016 (print) | LCC H62 (ebook) | DDC 300.72--dc23
LC record available at http://lccn.loc.gov/2015048876

Cover Photo Credit: Keren Weaver

Table of Contents

Acknowledgements vii

Chapter 1 1
Introduction and Background of the Project

Chapter 2 9
Inherent Challenges of Transdisciplinary Collaborations

Chapter 3 19
Data Troubles: Containment and Unruliness

Chapter 4 29
Toward a Methodology of Discomfort

Chapter 5 45
Crisis of Legitimation Magnified

Chapter 6 57
Audience Data Collection

Chapter 7 73
Curriculum

Chapter 8 85
Roads Ahead: Choosing Pathways of Discomfort and Humility

Appendices 95

Dedicated to Colonel David W. Sharp, Patricia Fairhead Sharp,
Connie Lunnen Durham, and John Wesley Durham, Jr.

ACKNOWLEDGEMENTS

The authors gratefully acknowledge the following entities from Texas Tech University: the Office of the Vice President for Research for Creative Arts, Humanities, and Social Sciences awards in 2012, 2013, and 2014; the School of Theatre and Dance for support and space; the College of Human Sciences Seed Grant. The authors also acknowledge the Anthony Marchionne Foundation for funding Elizabeth's wedding research and single women research, respectively. The authors thank Dr. Carl Bagley, Dr. Don Lavigne, Patrick DeCesaro, Dr. Sarah Atkins, Dr. Tom Blume, Rachel Ure, Liz Witmore, Dr. Kathleen Gillis, Keren Weaver, and Professor Kathryn Hollingsworth for their insights and support. The authors also acknowledge the following students in the College of Human Sciences at Texas Tech University for their support and assistance: Erika Brooks-Hurst, Jennifer Rojas McWhinney, Sam Christopher, Lauren Thompson, John Purcell, Ally Moreno, Victoria Heebner, Kellie Berkel-Hoffman, Kirsten Dalquist, and Christopher Asikis. We also thank Dr. Anisa Zvonkovic for her support of our Virginia Tech Scholars-Artists in Residence, and Drs. Libby Blume and Rosemary Weatherston for their support of our Scholars-Artists in Residence at the University of Detroit-Mercy. The authors are grateful to Texas Tech University and the University of Durham, UK, Institute of Advanced Study for time and resources to write the book. Finally, the authors offer their utmost appreciation to Flatlands Dance Theatre, and particularly Artistic Director Ali Duffy and Executive Director Kyla Olson, without whose support and participation this project would not have been possible.

Note about copyright: Portions of the text were taken from our published manuscripts, including:

Durham DeCesaro, Genevieve, and Elizabeth A. Sharp. "Almost Drowning: Data as a Troubling Anchor in a Dance/Social Science Collaboration." *International Journal of Qualitative Methods* 13 (2014): 411-421. Web. July 2014.

Durham DeCesaro, Genevieve, and Elizabeth A. Sharp. "Immersion in the Muddy Waters: A Collaboration Between a Social Scientist and a Dance Choreographer." *The International Journal of Social, Political and Community Agendas in the Arts* 7.3 (2014): 57-66. Web. January 2015.

Sharp, Elizabeth A. and Genevieve Durham DeCesaro. "Modeling Innovative Methodological Practices in a Dance/Family Studies Transdisciplinary Project." *Journal of Family Theory & Review* 7.4 (2015) 367–380. Print.

Sharp, Elizabeth A. and Genevieve Durham DeCesaro. "What Does Rejection Have to Do With it? Toward an Innovative, Kinesthetic Analysis of Qualitative Data." *Forum: Qualitative Social Research/Qualitative Sozialforschung* 14.2 (2013): n.pag August 2014.

CHAPTER 1

Introduction and Background of the Project

Image 1: Poster for the concert

Transdisciplinary projects are messy, complicated, and exhilarating. They offer potential to stretch the collaborators, sometimes uncomfortably, beyond their limits - beyond the predictable, expected, or routine. As it happens, though, the project we present in this book evolved from the germ of an idea that emerged while we were in the middle of something quite predictable, entirely expected, and uneventfully routine. The authors, one a choreographer and the other a social scientist, are not only colleagues at the same university, but are also running partners. For several years, we ran a set course at a set time on a set day of the week. During those runs, we'd talk about all manner of things, but more often than not, our discussions would return to the intersections of feminism with our academic identities and endeavors. Those discussions were informed by our experiences with our own weddings and marriages, including personally experiencing how contemporary social constructions of femininity continue to position marriage and motherhood as predictable, expected, and routine. Over the course of many miles, we began to lay the groundwork for a collaboration unlike anything either of us had ever done. At that point, it's fair to say that we didn't have any idea how very far our limits would be stretched!

It seems fitting, then, to introduce this book by diving right into an example of the complexity of transdisciplinary collaboration, focusing in particular on how challenging it can be to stretch our academic, disciplinary identities. This project used a kinesthetic analysis of social science qualitative data to create an hour-long professional dance performance. In between one of the dances, the choreographer wanted to use the following excerpt from the social science data:

> ...I had my wedding in a small town in Texas. It was a Saturday night...it was a garden wedding...it was outside. It was in May, and...my most memorable moment was getting kidnapped. It's family tradition that they kidnap the bride, and so all my cousins and my uncles, they tackled my husband, and then they grabbed me, and then they take me, you know, to get like a coke or something and bring me back, so it's fun.

The choreographer found this quote attention grabbing and provocative. She liked how it had the potential to encourage audiences to think more deeply about wedding rituals and how the practice of kidnapping women links to historical understandings and contemporary contexts. An "ordinary"—even trivial and funny (!)—wedding ritual of one woman's family playfully "kidnapping" the bride and "fake" attacking the groom maps onto an extraordinarily horrific occurrence of coveting women and women's bodies and taking women against their will.

The social scientist, though, did not want to use the quote in the performance (and did not use the quote in her data analysis—it was not germane to the analysis). The quote was elicited from a focus group (data collection) participant as a response to a "warm up" question and was not a particularly illuminating part of the young woman's narrative (she never discussed this again), nor did it connect with the 17 other participants in the study. Moreover, the social scientist did not like the vagueness in the description "*to get like a coke **or something**.*" The lack of specificity in this quote was problematic for the social scientist in her analysis. [1]

In our preferences and our rationales, we both drew on our distinct disciplinary training that were second nature to us after working in our disciplines for more than 20 years, respectively. The choreographer was privileging an expected theatrical/audience response and the social scientist was privileging a focus on the essence of participants' experiences and patterns in the dataset. Despite hearing the other's perspectives, neither one of us wanted to budge. We both thought we could persuade the other to "see it my way!" But that attitude turns out to be an approach that is counterproductive to transdisciplinary research.

---

[1] Typically, specific descriptions are better for analysis; nebulous statements are more difficult to code in qualitative analysis (e.g., Weiss, 1995).

This example is just one of many ways in which we disagreed in our project. In fact, our general disagreements became, over time, a rather ordinary component of our working process. Though we routinely held onto and promoted divergent perspectives and ways of approaching the project, eventually the culmination of these clashes led to some unexpected insights. Our growth, individually and as collaborators, has been extraordinary.

At the same time, while we have had remarkable experiences, there remains an ordinariness characterizing the project. For example, we used our routine, disciplinary analytic practices to approach the project and worked in our ordinary conditions, all the while examining and presenting features of (conventional) femininity often considered *ordinary*. It seems fitting, then, to explore the ways in which things that are often assumed to be ordinary (disciplinary paradigms, social expectations associated with being a woman) constitute complex, yet barely visible battlegrounds on which extended or even lifelong wars are fought in silence.

This book is an exploration of our project, from its inception through its current state, with a focus on providing interested readers and researchers with a understanding of and appreciation for the ways in which working collaboratively on a transdisciplinary project is at once incredibly challenging and unpredictably rewarding. In the book, we invite the reader backstage, exposing our discomfort, missteps, misgivings, confusion, exhilaration, successes, and lessons learned. Our project has been fraught with fears of distortion and dishonesty and punctuated with questions of truth, fiction, acts of commission, and acts of omission. It also has been accompanied by groundbreaking ideas, feelings of triumph, and exponential growth. We have continuously grappled with ontological, epistemological, methodological, and axial issues. We have engaged in disciplinary "gripping" (i.e., clinging to our distinct disciplinary training) and disciplinary "posturing" (i.e., privileging our disciplinary practices and hiding behind them)…until we finally moved to *disciplinary humility*. As the reader will learn, reaching a sense of *disciplinary humility* was slow going and painful. At times, it felt like a nearly impossible destination. It was only after we embraced our intense discomfort that we pulled our minds (and bodies) out of the metaphorical molasses of disciplinary gripping and posturing.

To orient the reader, in this introductory chapter we share a brief description of the project. In the succeeding chapters, we situate our project within the larger literature, exposing problems of classification that map onto broader challenges within the academy (Chapter 2). Following this, we bring into focus one of most troubling aspects of transdisciplinary work: data. We join other scholars in fundamentally questioning what data is, and we share how we came to terms with our data dilemmas (Chapter 3). Data dilemmas were central to our relentless discomfort working on the project and provide a background for our methodology of discomfort (Chapter 4). In Chapter 5, we take on complicated questions of how to evaluate a transdisciplinary project and share evaluative criteria we developed for our project. Whether we met the criteria is evidenced (partly) in the audience reactions we collected at all five performances; we excerpt a sampling of those reactions for the reader. Chapter 6 showcases our evolving process of collecting audience reactions and provides the reader with a broad overview of the audience responses to the performances. Chapter 7 highlights curricular frameworks to accompany the live performance and the video of the live performance. Finally, in Chapter 8, we close the book with our summarizing comments and ideas for future work.

OVERVIEW OF OUR TRANSDISCIPLINARY PROJECT

As mentioned previously, our project emerged from ordinary circumstances. We were on one of our early morning jogs when the choreographer proposed the idea of the project to the social scientist. Although we'd worked together for several years, that work was limited primarily to service at our university rather than collaborative research. Our shared interest in feminism and in publicizing women's narratives led us to discuss the possibility of applying to a new university-wide initiative encompassing the arts, humanities, and social sciences. That proposal resulted in a funded project titled: *Toward Innovative and Transdisciplinary Methodologies: Re-presenting Social Science Data Through Dance*. The project is based on the choreographer's kinesthetic analysis of two separate qualitative datasets, part of the social scientist's programmatic line of research examining women's relational lives (see social scientist's faculty profile for a listing of her publications: https://www.depts.ttu.edu/hs/hdfs/sharp.php).

We want to point out that the social scientist did not dance and that this project was a secondary data analysis, not a dissemination of the social scientist's findings. We bring this point forward because we have learned that when the social scientist tells others about her work with the choreographer, the assumption is that the goal of the project was to disseminate the social scientist's findings (we return to this in Chapter 2).

The initial project promised a fully-realized dance concert as the end product. We titled the dance concert *Ordinary Wars* because the research used as the stimulus for the performance captures women's routine, on-going negotiations with their (hegemonic) feminine and heterosexual identities within heteropatriarchal cultural conditions (S. Jackson). These negotiations are often couched as ordinary but are fraught with intense internal battles with societal expectations. *Ordinary Wars*, performed by members of Flatlands Dance Theatre, a professional, not-for-profit dance company (www.flatlandsdance.org), features six distinct dances interspersed with performed dialogues taken directly from the social scientist's interview data.

The dances were created from two separate datasets, which are, as previously noted, part of the social scientist's broader research program. The first dataset is from a constructivist grounded theory study examining 18 young women's weddings and transitions to being wives. Data were collected through two focus groups and individual interviews in a southwestern town in the United States. The other dataset is from a constructivist grounded theory study based on individual interviews with 35 women (in several cities in the United States) who did not want to marry and/or have children. For both projects, interviews were transcribed verbatim and audio recorded. The choreographer was provided with all transcripts (hard copies and electronic documents) and audio recordings.

Tallying the two datasets resulted in more than 1000 double-spaced pages of transcript data and 45 hours of audio recordings.

Our decision to work toward the goal of re-presenting data of women's experiences in ordinary conditions (e.g., transitioning to marriage, being single, thinking about motherhood) in an evening-length concert was measured. We observed that issues described by research participants in our project were: 1) commonly left out of community dialogues; 2) infrequently used as subject matter in contemporary (or historical) dance; and 3) given attention by researchers primarily in the academy, making such attention largely insular and inaccessible to women themselves and their home communities. The vision of the larger project is to affect change in our respective fields and in our communities through making visible what we have come to understand are extraordinary *Ordinary Wars*.

DESCRIPTION OF THE CONCERT

Ordinary Wars has been commissioned and performed five times[2], with more than 500 audience members having viewed the performance. The concert, which premiered in March 2013 (see Appendix E for a detailed description of the project prior to the concert premiere), includes six choreographed[3] dances: "I Was Happy in the Pictures;" "A Thin Line;" "Dressed (Parts 1 and 2);" "With Doubt;" "The Cowboy, the Lawyer, and the Stork;" and "To Find My Voice." Additionally, dialogues (performed by two actors in the first two performances and performed by one actor in the last three performances) featuring theatrical performance of original data from the social scientist's studies connect the six dances. The dialogues are performed in between all but one of the individual dances. After the final dance, "To Find My Voice," the performers participate in a concluding presentation titled "Brave." "Brave" is movement statement that includes oral and written presentation on the performers' bodies of verbatim portions of the transcript data (see final concert program in Appendix D).

The content of the concert was developed and arranged in order to both engage and challenge audiences. From her two decades of experience in dance, the choreographer understood that some audiences might disconnect from the concert if the material presented was too abstract. For that reason, in addition to several abstract dances, we decided to include data spoken narrative and several dances with linear narrative or clearly structured storylines (see Viewing the Concert, below, for additional information). Affording audiences some level of familiarity with what they are viewing is helpful in encouraging them to engage with, interpret, and dialogue about what they are seeing.

---

[2] The social scientist was unable to attend the first two performances of the fully-realized concert, as she was living and working in the UK. This was something that neither the social scientist nor the choreographer had anticipated and we discuss it in more detail in Appendix E.

[3] The term "choreographer," unless otherwise indicated in this manuscript, refers to the lead choreographer. Two additional choreographers, both affiliated with Flatlands Dance Theatre, created a total of three dances out of the six included in the final concert structure.

Inspired by discussions of sensory ethnography (e.g., Pink), we created interactive opportunities for our audiences. For example, when audience members entered the lobby area prior to a performance, they were greeted with information about the creation of the concert, our backgrounds and the background of the project, and our larger research agenda (see Image 2). In addition, during the intermission, audience members had the option to eat a white cupcake (see Image 3) served on a napkin (see Image 4); the napkins were printed with data related to the two social science studies; for example, one napkin read: "44% of U.S. adults are single. 1,138 benefits are given to married people." Our intention here was to encourage audiences to question an ordinary ritual at weddings (consumption of cake). We intended for audience members to contemplate what they were "biting into" when tasting products typically associated with marriage as a largely heteronormative institution.

Finally, after the concert, audience members were asked to complete a written survey about the concert and were encouraged to stay for a post-concert discussion to share their reactions to the performance. In the first three concerts, the audience was invited to stay for a focus group and in the latter two concerts, audience members were invited to a "hybrid" focus group/talkback session. As we share in Chapter 6, we decided to modify the data collection after the performance because we encountered difficulties with getting audience members to participate in the focus groups (a data collection strategy common in social sciences but not in dance). With iterations of the concert, we have refined our approaches to the presentations using data collected from audience members at the preceding performances.

VIEWING THE CONCERT

To help further orient readers, we suggest they watch the video of the inaugural live performance, performed by Flatlands Dance Theatre in Lubbock, Texas in March 2013. Viewing the performance before reading Chapters 2-7 promises to help readers more readily digest and appreciate the ideas and arguments we present. We also recommend readers consider watching the video a second time, after finishing the book. Re-watching the video is likely to encourage readers to forge deeper links and more fully comprehend the complexity of transdisciplinary work. To view the performance, we invite the reader to: www.ordinarywars.org.

Introduction and Background of the Project 7

Image 2: Lobby posters with information about the project and research process

Image 3: Cupcakes available in the lobby during intermission.

Image 4: Napkins available at the cupcake table: the napkins are printed with statistics.

CHAPTER 2

Inherent Challenges of Transdisciplinary Collaborations

"Is it too simple of a response to say this is 'social science' and 'tis is not social science'" (Kip Jones', 2012, in his introduction about his film based on qualitative data.)

Image 5: "I Was Happy in the Pictures," taken at March 2013 performance, Lubbock, Texas

To help situate a primary source of the clashes and disagreements in our transdisciplinary project, we bring attention to the larger bifurcation of academic disciplines. Institutions of higher education rely on categorical, disciplinary distinctions in order to function. While a single faculty member may share a joint appointment in two or more disciplines, those each have names (e.g., Biology, English) and corresponding identities, expectations, and practices. Our experiences with *Ordinary Wars* suggest that collaborations like ours are challenging to fund, to support, and to promote because they question the relevance of disciplinary distinctions to the value of a research process and its associated product.

Literature on collaboration within the academy provides insight into questions of disciplinary structures and embedded identities. A fair number of descriptions concern collaborations that are highly structured and designed to allow individuals with different areas of expertise to contribute their respective expertise to a product. In his essay on collaboration in higher education, Roger

Baldwin (27) proposes that, independent of any institutional initiatives, individuals collaborate because they are motivated by "increasing prestige or influence, sharing resources and reducing costs, and facilitating learning." We suggest adding a fourth motivation, "facilitating transformative change," primarily so that "facilitating learning" might include an action statement. Our own motivation is most aligned with facilitating transformative change, but this is entirely dependent on facilitating learning.

Baldwin and Chang list a series of prescriptions designed both to inform future collaborators how to approach collaboration and to provide an overview of ways in which collaborations in higher education are challenging and/or successful. Other authors (e.g., Austin and Baldwin) offer various kinds of procedures for different groups (administrators, researchers, junior faculty members) interested in pursuing collaboration in academic environments. Missing from these reviews are descriptions of how collaborators negotiate their conflicts in nuanced and sustained ways. As Hodgins and Boydell note in a written conversation about arts-based health research: "There is so much written descriptively about the content and form of such research but very little critical thought focused on the theoretical, methodological and ethical challenges encountered by the scientists, artists and trainees engaged in conducting these projects."

Kezar (809) would take this a step further, arguing that not only must *researchers* (Kezar's emphasis) shift their focus to their processes, but also that *institutions* must be transformed in order to facilitate successful collaborations. As Kezar notes, there is little research that analyzes processes of (academic) collaboration, and the research that does exist fails to explore the "systemic elements" of traditional, collaborative structures within the academy.

The lack of process-based analysis of collaborations within the academy reveals a tendency to understand collaborations as methodologically prescriptive and to associate their value with the production of a tangible artifact: a product. This stipulates that the end-goal of any collaboration should include the production of *something*. We offer that working to publicize processes of collaboration in higher education gives value to the ways in which those processes can be effective mechanisms for systematic, structural change. This is not to suggest that the categorical organization supplied by disciplinary distinctions is in need of a complete overhaul; rather, we recommend that structural change center around the ways in which university communities understand the value of collaborations, even those with no defined product.

As we embarked on our own project, then, we committed to acknowledging, troubling, and publicizing our process. We contend that doing so helps establish a precedent for privileging processes of collaborative projects along with the products. It is important to situate both components equally so that the processes become an integral part of the dialogue on collaboration within the academy, which, in turn, promotes an awareness of the ways in which structural boundaries (such as disciplinary paradigms) function in research.

Processes of Collaboration

A necessary first step in publicizing our process was to describe it using current and effective language. This meant gathering information on labels used to describe the structures of collaborative practices and the methodologies those practices promote.

Integrated disciplinary efforts within the academy are generally described as inter (or multi), cross, and/or trans-disciplinary. Although these terms are frequently used interchangeably, there are important distinctions among them; we draw on Paul Jeffrey's overview (540-541) of collaborations with more than one discipline. He qualifies both inter and crossdisciplinary research as involving individuals from distinct disciplines working toward a defined goal using their own disciplinary practices and maintaining their respective disciplinary paradigms. Generally, cross and interdisciplinary projects lack substantive disciplinary integration, though Jeffrey offers that there is a push in interdisciplinary work for collaborators to integrate their disciplinary practices and paradigms for the benefit of the project. In contrast, transdisciplinary research is characterized by meaningful synthesis of disciplinary ways of knowing and doing, resulting in the development of practices unique to the project.

Transdisciplinary research is new enough that it provides researchers with few standard guidelines and limited resolutions about rigor, process, or products. Indeed, an exhaustingly high level of ambiguity characterizes transdisciplinary work. Collaborative researchers Gergen and Gergen, in their book *Playing with Purpose: Adventures in Performative Social Science (Writing Lives)*, describe their work with both the arts and the sciences as inhabiting liminoid space. This is another way of understanding the ambiguity encompassing transdisciplinary research; it creates a condition of continuous questioning of one's disciplinary theories and practices. For example: How do disciplinary practices work within a transdisciplinary project? Does blurring disciplinary boundaries delegitimize the work in question? If so, how? And, what are the ethical stakes in transdisciplinary research?

Having situated our collaboration firmly within a liminoid space, we worked to clarify our methodological approach. This task required reviewing what seemed to be a veritable flood of potential labels, all attempting to qualify inter, cross, and/or transdisciplinary collaborations involving the arts.

Complications with Categorization

Numerous labels for projects seeking to combine, integrate, and/or borrow aspects of social science and the arts exist in the literature. These include but are not limited to "art-based research" (McNiff); "arts-based research" (Finley); "performative social science" (Gergen and Jones); "arts-oriented research" (Gergen and Gergen, *Playing*); "performed research" (LaFreniere et al,); "aesthetic methods" (Piercy and Benson); "arts-informed research" (Knowles and Cole), "performance inquiry" (Gergen and Gergen, "Mischief"), "performed ethnography" (Alexander), and "research with a performance orientation" (Gergen and Gergen, "Mischief"). (See Table 1 for a concise overview.) The two most frequently used terms are "arts-based research" and "performative social science." While we provide overviews of each, we would note that our work does not fit precisely within either. This is problematic because of the way that categorization functions in higher education.

Categorical identifiers (disciplines, titles, departments) in the academy function to situate what we do and who we are into fairly universally understood descriptions. These same identifiers also, we argue, assign value to us and to our work. One of the reasons we advocate an investigation of categorical identity at the outset of transdisciplinary collaborations is that the labels collaborators give themselves and their work will frame how the work is heard, read, viewed, and valued.

Table 1: Overview of Terminology
Juxtaposition Table for Variant Performative Social Science Labels (N = 9)

Label	Definition
Art-based Research	"Art-based research can be defined as the systematic use of the artistic process, the actual making of artistic expressions in all of the different forms of the arts, as a primary way of understanding and examining experience by both researchers and the people that they involve in their studies." (McNiff 29)
Arts-based Research[a]	"Arts-based research describes an epistemological foundation for human inquiry that utilizes artful ways of understanding and representing the worlds in which research is constructed." (Finley 79)
Performative Social Science[a]	"Any social research or human inquiry that adapts the tenets of the creative arts as a part of the methodology," (Jones and Leavy 1)
Aesthetic Methods	"Methods of presentation that call for a more evocative, interpretive response from the reader or audience, another level of reflection and meaning making (sometimes hand-in-hand with raw data, and sometimes not)." (Piercy and Benson 109)
Arts-informed Research	"Arts-informed research is a mode and form of qualitative research in the social sciences that is influenced by, but not based in, the arts broadly conceived." (Cole and Knowles 59)
Performance Ethnography	"Performance ethnography is literally the staged re-enactment of ethnographically derived notes." (Alexander 75)

[a]The two most frequently used terms are "arts-based research" and "performative social science." The authors' work does not fit precisely within either genre.

As we began to create the framework for what is now our full concert, we faced a crisis of categorization in terms of what to call the process that led to its creation. If we labeled the concert "social science," what would that evoke? How would the social science label focus audience members' gazes? How would the social science classification orient the consumers of our research? Would they look for "real" stories, "real" experiences, a systematic analysis, and minimal subjectivity? Would they make assumptions about the processes employed to reach the product? By the same token, if we called our product a dance, what would this evoke? How would the gaze shift? Would consumers have fewer concerns with "real" stories? Would they focus less on narratives? Might there be a greater propensity for openness to interpretation, art, and emotion? Conversely, would there be less validity or legitimacy, particularly in an academic or research context?

What about the labels "social science dance" or "danced social science" or "dancing the data" as Bagley and Cancienne termed their work together? What might these classifying devices mean and could they work as possible labels for our project? Do we have something that is *not wholly* dance and *not wholly* social science? If so, does this mean we are relegated to the margins of our own disciplines or, more positively, that we are creating a critical space for work that has potential to live simultaneously in both fields? Have we created something that is *more* than dance and *more* than social science?

This tension of categorization is illustrated in an example from National Public Radio's (NPR) retraction of an episode of "This American Life" that originally aired in January of 2012. NPR formally retracted the episode on March 16, 2012. The original episode featured Mike Daisey, the writer and performer of a one-man show called "The Agony and The Ecstasy of Steve Jobs," about Apple's treatment of workers in China. Daisey had advertised his play as based on his research from his travels to China ("truth") and, based on this information, NPR had promoted Daisey's play as "truth." It was later revealed that some information in Daisey's play was not accurate. Daisey had embellished parts of the story and said he had witnessed events that he had not (although he had heard about the events). The question became: was it a work of truth *or* a work of fiction that had some truth to it? NPR, in its retraction, questioned Daisey's ethics by stating that he "lied" to that organization, particularly the program called "This American Life" and its audiences. Daisey, in turn, stated the following: "My mistake, the mistake I truly regret, is that I had it on your show as journalism, and it's not journalism. It's theater" (Peralta).

When the social scientist listened to the NPR program her stomach was in knots. She became slightly paranoid and envisioned herself as Daisey—being publically admonished for mislabeling the collaborative project if she kept social science in the label! She questioned her role and the data's role in the process, raising concerns such as: "Do I have any power? Does the data in my datasets have any power*? Do I have a right to offer limits to the choreographers' and performers' freedom to respond to and enact the data? Do I have veto power in a project like this? Will the data be closely consulted and how will I be able to discern this?" [*Note this question launched the social scientist into debates about the post-humanist turn (Braidotti).]

In contrast to the social scientist, the choreographer was not *initially* troubled by how they would publicize their work together. Dance choreography and performance are subjective endeavors. While, in some cases, choreographers work from notated scores in order to recreate "accurate" historic dances, the ideas of rightness and/or accuracy are not central to the development or production of dance. Instead, as described by seminal American dance choreographer Doris Humphrey (and others), interpretation, craft, and artistic integrity are prioritized as guiding structural principles for dance-making (Humphrey). The choreographer anticipated that her choreography might be evaluated according to these (or other) principles generally associated with dance-making, but she did not expect that her dances would be questioned based on whether they accurately represented the data.

It is clear that categorization is a critical component of how research and its associated products are received. Further, choosing to categorize our work within an existing discipline acknowledges, at some level, that our work can be evaluated according to standards and expectations of that discipline. An easy fix would simply be to come up with a new and ingenious term for our transdisciplinary collaboration. We follow Barone and Eisner in our hesitation to discard entirely the very terms that seem to get us in the most hot water.

Briefly, Barone and Eisner argue that approaches like ours *should* claim categorical labels like *social science* and *research* precisely because of what those labels imply within the academy (45). Their recommendation is that projects like ours, in claiming these terms, can work to publicize the ways in which the terms themselves have become so tied to assumptions of expectations and value that they have become less about describing ways of working/types of work and more about maintaining institutional hierarchies that promote exclusion and binary thinking. With this in mind, we highlight two of the labels that, at least in current literature, are most commonly used to describe projects that bear some similarity to ours: arts-based research and performative social science.

ARTS-BASED RESEARCH

The term arts-based research is often used to describe research collected or disseminated using arts practices, such as having participants listen to music and/or having participants create pictures and/or using music or art in intervention programs. As Goldstein, Gray, Salisbury, and Snell note, practices like these have gained traction in the academy because "they provide researchers with particularly rich ways to collect, analyze, and share research" (675). However, most of the literature describes research processes that either gather data specifically for the purpose of using the data in an artistic way (Leavy) or that use artistic tools to disseminate the data. Pariser, in a particularly useful analysis of arts-based research, explores both of these approaches.

Pariser, citing Bean [1], presents provocative arguments about arts-based research, several of which are critical to showcasing complexities of arts and

---

[1] Bean offers a compelling overview of ways in which research has been understood in Western philosophy and provides distinctions about how research functions *in* the arts.

social science partnerships. Pariser elaborates on Bean's conclusion that there exists a "fundamental disjunction" (2) between research practices of artists and scientists; our understanding of his claim is that the research practices used by artists are not only different than those used by scientists, they do not constitute legitimate research. While we agree with *part of* Pariser's observation, specifically that the research practices of artists and scientists (and any other group) may differ, we would caution against reifying the binary between arts and sciences, one that usually positions the arts in a subordinated role. Pariser explains that to describe both practices as research "does a disservice" (3) to both the arts and the sciences. This begs more scrutiny, as does his claim that, among other fairly negative attributes, "arts-based research is neither good research nor good art" (9).

What Pariser claims is troublesome and suggests that there is no room for developing disciplinary practices and expectations specific to the genre of arts-based research. This implication is central to our own work, as we find that it is reflected in audience responses to our publications, presentations, and the concert itself. We have encountered a distinct preference in the audiences for our scholarly publications and presentations to want to classify our transdisciplinary project either as social science *or* as dance; we observe, in our audiences, a reluctance to consider the possibility of trying to define new methodologies specific to a way of researching that is not wholly one thing or the other.

We would advocate that Barone and Eisner's *Arts Based Research* is an effective counter to some of Pariser's conclusions, though Pariser works very hard in his own right to deconstruct Eisner's earlier publications. Barone and Eisner promote an understanding of arts-based research that we think is the most inclusive of the diversity of projects that claim this moniker: they write that "arts based research is an effort to extend beyond the limiting constraints of discursive communication in order to express meanings that otherwise would be ineffable" (1). This perspective is substantiated by the actual title, in *Dancing the Data* (Bagley and Cancienne), of Donald Blumenfeld-Jones' essay: "If I Could Have Said It, I Would Have."

This understanding takes the concept of value off the table. Barone and Eisner focus, instead, on how different kinds of communication might be suited for different kinds of research. Instead of comparing the rigor and value of "arts" to the rigor and value of "research," they promote the idea that "matters of meaning are shaped...by the tools we use" (1). This is a key point: it opens the door to consider whether traditional modes of presenting research (i.e., conference papers, publications, invited talks) best serve *all* research if the meaning of the research in question is in fact better suited to another mode of communication.

As described in Chapter 1, a focus of our project has been to publicize ways that women experience and understand particular expectations of femininity(ies). That idea of publicizing, or making space, for dialogue is dependent upon our audiences *noticing* these expectations to begin with. Barone and Eisner would agree that emphasizing the importance of noticing is a critical contribution of arts-based research. The value of our project is ultimately dependent on our ability to address "complex and often subtle interactions" in the data (in this example, that data is societal expectations of femininity) and create re-representations (in our cases, dances) "of those interactions in ways that make them noticeable" (2).

We return to Pariser here in order to further support our understanding of the purpose of arts-based research. Pariser's arguments are based largely on a perception that the purpose of arts-based research is the same as traditional research, which is—at least in part—to make claims about how things were, are, or might be and to disseminate those claims. Pariser also stipulates that valid research *must* rely on empirical substantiation of claims. This is clear when he writes that arts-based research can "only offer the promise of 'credibility'. That is, the work will seem believable" (11). This statement belies an assumption that valid research is defined and encountered in the narrowest of ways and, as such, is readily associated with some academic disciplines and not with others.

Our project, though, is not about making claims. Rather, it is about making public. In our case, this means getting audiences to talk about what they see in our concert; we encourage this by including talkback sessions after every performance. The value of our work, then, is not about what we have or have not claimed relative to existing "facts," but whether we have initiated engagement with and inquiry into our original subject: women's experiences with cultural notions of femininities. We suggest that arts-based research does not exist to answer questions but to ask them.

The term research-based art is less widely used than arts-based research, but we include it here as it could also describe our project. Barone and Eisner make the distinction that research-based art is that which uses research as the foundation for making art. This somewhat describes our project, at least in its most initial stages. We do not, though, entirely fit the model, as our art-work, the *Ordinary Wars* concert, never exists wholly separate from the research. It is a part of ongoing research that continues to define the concert itself.

Neither research-based art nor arts-based research leave adequate room for projects that volley back and forth, using both approaches almost simultaneously with a focus on reciprocity rather than dichotomy. What is the correct term, for example, when the research-based art (say, one of the six original dances created using social science data as their "bases") leads to questions that end up guiding and informing more traditional, written research? This is rather like the chicken and egg conundrum, in that it is very difficult, once involved, to separate out the "research" from the "art."

Performative Social Science

Gergen and Gergen ("Mischief") and others have argued that the social sciences are currently in the "performative turn." The label 'performative social science' (an umbrella term, broadly defined as the use of arts in the social sciences) emerged in the early 2000s, although the practice of using arts and social science research has been documented since the 1980s (Gergen and Gergen, "Performative"). The most innovative work has occurred within the last two decades. While the "performative turn" may be in its infancy in particular fields (e.g., Family Studies), in other social science fields, there are indicators of a growing acceptance of or willingness to experiment with the arts: the American Psychological Association held symposiums on performance social science in the late 1990's; in 2008, the *Forum: Qualitative Social Research* devoted an entire special issue (42 articles) to challenges and innovations of performative social science (see Jones and Leavy). In that special issue, for example, scholars wrote about their engagement with poetry, videos, art exhibits, performance work, photography, and the process of working with artists. Additionally, the *Qualitative Inquiry* journal (volume 20, issue 2) and *The International Review of Qualitative Research* (Summer 2014, volume 7) both recently published special issues on the arts and social sciences. Gergen and Jones went so far as to say that there "seems to be an explosion of interest in all of the arts and their possibilities within social science and more academics are beginning to explore their own creativity" (1).

While we are fairly closely aligned with the label performative social science, the progression of our research has given rise to reservations about applying this label to our work without some accompanying caveats or explanations. This is due largely to the ways in which popular perceptions of performative social science conceive of the role of the arts (and artists) in these projects. Guiney, for example, offers that "performative, in the widest sense of the word, has become a 'working title' for the efforts of social science researchers who are exploring the use of tools from the arts in research itself and/or using them to enhance, or move beyond PowerPoint conference presentations or traditional journal submissions in their dissemination efforts" (Guiney et al.). This would suggest that the arts are little more than tools to be used by the researcher; the arts are stripped of agency and artistic practices are relegated to vehicles for information distribution. Kip Jones (Jones and Leavy), in a written conversation with Patricia Leavy, explicitly affirms Guiney's conception of the term performative social science, writing, "I define PSS as the use of tools from the Arts in carrying out Social Science research and/or disseminating its findings" (1). Leavy, in response to Jones, offers a slightly more reciprocal perspective, stating that she understands performative social science as, '...any social research or human inquiry that adapts the tenets of the creative arts as a part of the methodology" (1).

While Leavy's definition is particularly in tune with our project, we offer that the label of performative social science, in general, implies using the arts toward a social science end (i.e., the researchers are, essentially, *performing* social science). Our project, though, is not a dissemination of the social scientist's findings. In other words, we did not embark upon this collaboration for the social scientist to share her analysis of the data (i.e., findings) and have those findings performed in a dance concert. To this end, we cannot wholly embrace the term performative social science to describe our project. Likewise, while arts-based research, as conceived by Barone and Eisner, *does* promote our project's fundamental values, it is broad and arguably invites criticism from individuals who contest the viability of arts practices as research. We therefore describe our work as a transdisciplinary project involving dance and social science. While a bit bulky, this most clearly and accurately describes what we are doing without relying on potentially loaded terms that might carry with them prescriptive and unwanted meanings. In our next chapter, we continue to explore the disciplinary prescriptions associated with relatively standard terminology and turn our focus to the word data, examining how our shifting understandings of data operated in our transdisciplinary project.

CHAPTER 3

Data Troubles: Containment and Unruliness

Image 6: "Dressed (Part 2)," taken at March 2013 performance, Lubbock, Texas

What is data? Contemporary definitions include: "facts and statistics collected together for reference or analysis." Synonyms include: information, intelligence, material, input. Distinguishing between what is data and what is not seems simple, but the social scientist found making this distinction increasingly difficult as she grew more involved in the transdisciplinary project.

At the start of the project, the social scientist clearly defined data as the material that had been collected/gathered from participants in her two studies: (A) brides/new wives and (B) single women. The data for the basis of this project were the audio files and transcripts (transcribed verbatim from the audio files) that the social scientist handed over/surrendered to the lead choreographer. The social scientist also considered the interviews with dancers, focus groups, audience surveys, and "talkback sessions" as data.

All of this seemed straightforward enough. Complications arose, though, after an unsuccessful "data" collection attempt at the third performance of the concert. Although we had trouble collecting data from the first two performances, our third performance was definitely the worst in terms of survey completion/return rate and focus group participation. We tried text messaging as a means of gathering data and received some text responses at the third performance; however, the response rate was very low (i.e., we received seven completed responses via text out of a total of approximately 100 participating audience members). Adding to that, we received no paper surveys, nor did anyone volunteer for the focus group. The social scientist expressed concern and lamented to the choreographer that so little data had been collected from the performance.

A noteworthy conversation ensued. The choreographer asked the social scientist to open up her understanding of "data." She wrote in an email: "At any rate, the performance was very successful...and we didn't need surveys or text messages to validate the success of the performance." It is important to note here that the social scientist was not looking to the data to *validate* the performance; she was interested in the audience members' reactions—feelings and interpretations in response to the concert. The choreographer, though, interpreted her colleague's need for data as evidence to validate the "success of the performance." The choreographer thought that the social scientist did not feel like a performance of the concert was successful if it did not yield adequate data. This misunderstanding describes a clear distinction between how both researchers conceived of data.

In response to the choreographer's statement that the performance "felt" successful to the dancers, the social scientist responded: "It does sound like there was amazing energy there and, in the end, perhaps the texting would have distracted the audience members from their enjoyment of the performance. I definitely wanted to email the performers this weekend to hear their perspectives but I paused because I felt that some of them think the research (and documentation) is distracting (and/or devaluing?) from their work and the performance itself." The choreographer responded: "This is part of the argument about "what is data?" I would like to make the case that even though we didn't have surveys, we had the audience engaged and committed and the performers feeling the energy...and this tells us something important."

This exchange encouraged the social scientist to ask herself: am I being too narrow in my understanding of data? Can we capture the atmosphere of the space and consider that data? Should I consider the energy and receptivity of the crowd instead of only asking about the audience member's individual reactions to the performance in a survey? Should I look to the dancers' impressions/feelings about the performance? Are the dancers' bodies data in and of themselves?

Before we grapple with these questions, we will first share with the reader how we initially and distinctly approached the "easily agreed upon" data- the data from the social scientists' qualitative studies. We offer a wider framing of how we each encounter and conceptualize data in the context of this project—what we are calling our relationships with the datasets.[1]

Relationships with Data

The social scientist's relationship to the data in our project can be characterized as close, valued and contextualized. It is fair to say that because of her training as a social scientist, data has a privileged position for her—she makes most decisions based on data. In her analysis for her social science publications, for example, the

---

[1] The subsections "Relationships with Data" and "Analytic Practices" were originally published by the authors in the *Journal of Family Theory & Review* and are used here with permission.

social scientist closely reads the data, engaging in line-by-line coding (Charmaz). It is typical for her to read transcripts more than five times each. She writes summaries about each participant, reflecting on what is shared in the interview and the conditions of the interview. The extent to which she depends on and privileges data was made evident in her work with this project. This awareness has helped her question how such (rigid) dependence can be a hindrance in a transdisciplinary project and in her own work.

Many times, but not always, choreographers use data and other stimuli (text, visual images, political situations) as "jumping off" points. For the choreographer's role in this project, she presumed she could read the transcripts once, "pull" the excerpts that she thought would be most fruitful in terms of theatrical re-presentation, and begin to develop choreography. The choreographer did not anticipate that the social scientist would be so familiar with the data that she would question when the choreographer made artistic decisions that did not accurately re-present the environment or the context of the original interview in the datasets.

Both of us thought we were addressing conflicts that emerged from our different relationships with the data when we discussed the ethics of artistic license with respect to re-presentation of data. We discovered, though, that a more complex issue underlying our conflicts was actually one of disciplinary identities. We each privileged our own learned ways of knowing and doing in the context of approaching the data rather than working to creatively and collaboratively devise new methodologies for a transdisciplinary analysis. Below, we briefly share our separate (and disciplinarily "safe") analyses of/approaches to the datasets.

ANALYTIC PRACTICES: SOCIAL SCIENCE

The social scientist used a modified constructivist grounded theory approach (Charmaz) to examine the data. Charmaz' adaptation of grounded theory methodology draws from both postmodernism and post-positivism sensibilities. The analytic technique is primarily inductive/emergent whereby the analysis addresses participants' ideas, behaviors, and interactions present in the data.

The social scientist conducted (or facilitated the conduction of) focus group interviews, focus group debriefing sessions, and individual interviews. These were all transcribed verbatim. Memos (researcher's analytic musings and questions) about group dynamics of each focus group were typed and inserted at the end of transcripts. The social scientist became immersed in the data over several months. As she analyzed, she continually asked: "What am I learning? What are the participants saying/expressing?" and "Am I doing justice to their stories?" She attempted to keep an open mind throughout the analytic process.

The social scientist listened to audio recordings multiple times, read interviews multiple times, coded line by line, and later refined the coding and began abstracting. Charmaz recommends that researchers consciously use gerunds when coding, thereby emphasizing the ways in which participants are active in their narratives. The social scientist also drew on Lloyd, Emery and Klatt's analytic practices. Lloyd et al. recommend identifying larger discourses operating and searching for instances of both compliance/collusion with and resistance to larger discourses. The social scientist's analysis focused on contradictions, gendered enactment, and identity, in an effort to be conscious of the homogenous experiences women were discussing as well as the diverse positions of the participants (e.g., age, cost of the wedding, etc.). As the social scientist analyzed the data, she considered how larger structures (e.g., "bridezilla"[2]), were operating in participants' expressions (Risman).

To provide additional insight into her process of analysis, the social scientist draws on examples from one of the studies—the wedding study. She began examining data by developing a single descriptive indicator capturing the first emergent idea (e.g., stopped planning the wedding) and then proceeded to examine more data, comparing the indicator in the new data to the initial indicator. If the data did not fit within the existing indicator(s), a new indicator was developed (e.g., "asserting my desires for a small wedding"). This process continued until all data were analyzed. The indicators were then grouped into concepts, which are labels associated with several indicators. For example, indicators of "stopped planning the wedding" and "asserting my desires for a small wedding" were part of the concept "managing/responding to wedding stress." Categories were then developed by classifying concepts, with the social scientist asking, "How are the concepts fitting together?" Categories that were developed reflect an integration of the participants' explanations/descriptions and the social scientist's interpretations (DeSantis and Ugarriza).

ANALYTIC PRACTICES: DANCE

The choreographer analyzed the data by exploring its potential for re-presentation through dance and/or in a theatrical concert. Her approach is fundamentally different from social scientists' interactions with qualitative data. Choreographers foreground the body and do not set out to "represent experience but to find aesthetic insight about the experience" (Knowles and Cole 176). As Blumenfeld-Jones explains in *Dancing the Data* (Bagley and Cancienne), "I 'see' what strikes me, what seems to have potential to go somewhere" (95). He argues that in his own collaborative projects, the meaning of a dance is not established by the data (words) he reads, but rather by the dance itself and the process of its creation (95).

The choreographer generated choreography by using the data as a starting point. She began by reading the transcripts while simultaneously listening to the audio recordings of the transcripts. However, she quickly, and in conversation with the social scientist, jettisoned the audio recordings because she found that the tonal qualities in the participants' voices were negatively influencing her engagement with/analysis of the data. As the choreographer stated to the social scientist during a recorded conversation:

> I was expecting to hear [on the audio recordings] this performed transcript... Maybe because I had an eye toward what our final performance project was going to look and sound like. [Instead], I was

---

2 In the United States, "bridezilla" is a colloquial term used to describe a bride who is considered overly demanding.

> hearing this really casual, jocular, and some of them I would classify as very 'valley-girl-ish' and I didn't want to hear it, I didn't want to hear it, I didn't want to hear it, so I stopped.

The choreographer also noted to the social scientist in an email communication that reading the transcripts without listening to the accompanying audio gave her more "freedom in approaching the data...in connecting with it on a personal and experiential level."

Once the choreographer made the decision to analyze the data without listening to the audio recordings of the transcripts, she turned her focus to "mining" the data[3] for its kinesthetic possibilities. Her use of this term is akin to the manual process of mining for rare gems; it suggests the data is the root source of the choreography; she "mined" it by digging through it for these metaphorical "gems" (ideas/images/words) that she was able to extract. The choreographer did this in two ways. She responded to some transcripts or sections thereof by journaling about the content she read and describing kinesthetic reactions to it. The choreographer used this approach primarily in the dance "Dressed," though it did inform some of her artistic decisions (e.g., music choices, overall intention of the dances) in both "I Was Happy in the Pictures" and "To Find My Voice." Following is an excerpt from the choreographer's records that illustrates this means of analysis:

> There is a great sadness to [the data]. It makes me think of shoulders pressed down and upper body curved. Like a woman crushed under the weight of it all. There is a great story here about finding freedom only to discover the freedom was an illusion, or at least that the freedom is much different than expected.

In the excerpt above, the choreographer described kinesthetic connections with the data: she began by qualifying the data in question as "sad," then continued by physicalizing the idea of sadness with the additional description of being weighed down by social expectations. At this point, the choreographer went into the dance studio and began working to develop what are called movement "motifs" using her physical descriptions of the data to guide her. In choreography, motifs are movements or movement sequences that form the backbone of a dance. They are usually repeated throughout the work, though are manipulated from their original form.

A second means of kinesthetic analysis involved using specific words or phrases from the data to build choreographic motifs. The choreographer used this approach in the dance "I Was Happy in the Pictures." Most of the primary motifs in this dance were created using six statements from the data:

1. It's a lot harder than what I thought it was going to be.
2. The yellow roses were gorgeous.

---

[3] Mining the data, as the choreographer used the term, should not be confused with data mining, which is generally understood as the practice of analyzing large databases to generate information.

3. So I wasn't like giddy or blissful or anything like that and I'm not sure why exactly I just wasn't.
4. You can tell that I was happy in the pictures, you know it's not a fake smile.
5. As soon as we were married my love for him increased greatly and I don't know why I guess.
6. And I kinda felt like I had an identity crisis a little bit (laughing). I mean not really by any means but it kinda felt like I got lost in what X [my husband] wanted.

This type of analysis was also used for the dance "To Find My Voice," though for this dance, the choreographer did not select data phrases due to their kinesthetic potential but because she and the social scientist determined (using pilot performance data as evidence) that singlehood was being muted in the concert. In response, the choreographer and social scientist worked together to select data phrases that explicitly commented on singlehood; the choreographer then used those phrases to build the dance's motifs.

JOINT ANALYSIS (THE EMERGENCE OF CRISIS MODE)[4]

Our understanding of each other's analytic practices has consistently challenged us. The ways in which we analyzed/read the original data emerged as a recurring locus of questions and confusion in our collaboration. The choreographer, as described in the previous section, used journaling, bodily experience, lived experience, and personal reactions as analytic tools. The choreographer was fully comfortable with the idea that the intimacy of choreography necessitated an intimate treatment of the data in which her own experiences reading the data were as important as the data itself. The social scientist, on the other hand, privileged participants' experiences over her own.

Both approaches were particularly valuable as independent practices of analysis but did not lend themselves to an easy and clear integration. There was a general murkiness surrounding how our distinct approaches would be perceived by the other in terms of both legitimacy and ethics, and how the two analytic approaches would eventually come together - would it be possible for two approaches to mutually inform each other and create a "hybrid" (or third) analysis, or would it be necessary to privilege one analysis over the other?

Embarking on the project, the social scientist wavered between post-positivism, constructionism, and critical paradigms. Although she finds constructivism and critical paradigms appealing, her training in post-positivism occasionally reared its (ugly) head as we worked our way through this project. For example, the social scientist assumed that the choreographer would use an aggregate understanding/command of each data set—that is, she would choreograph based on patterns *across* participants. In the early stages of this project, the choreographer was working to develop choreography for "I Was

---

[4] The subsection "Joint Analysis" was originally published by the authors in the *International Journal of Qualitative Methods* and is used here with permission.

Happy in the Pictures," briefly described in the previous section. The choreographer filmed a draft version of that dance, performed by three women, and sent it[5] to the social scientist for review. After viewing the dance, the social scientist discovered that the data the choreographer used as stimuli were all from one participant (out of 18). As the social scientist shared this with the choreographer, it became clear that the choreographer had not considered it a crucial component of her analysis.

Social Scientist:
> I just discovered that all the data excerpts are from one participant. Now, I am more confused—why three women and why not one? Or is it that the women are the same woman, at different stages? Maybe dancer 1 is helping herself when dancers 2 and 3 lead dancer 1 back?

Choreographer:
> This goes back to me not really thinking about WHERE the quotes were coming from. I do like the idea, though, of exploring the suggestion that a single woman is "allowed" or "socially permitted" to have multiple identities during her wedding: innocent (white) bride, "bridezilla," neurotic bride, ecstatic bride, weepy bride, etc. Again, this might be something to talk about as an ethics issue. Do I have a responsibility to the data to keep it intact in terms of its origins?

It is interesting to note that the choreographer's response did not contain the same urgency (in terms of concern for representation of more than one participant from the data) as the social scientist's initial question. The choreographer fairly quickly moved away from the social scientist's expressed concern and introduced her own questions about artistic license in a project like this. The following excerpt reinforces the social scientist's focus on questioning the role of *context* in relationship to the data used by the choreographer and affirms the choreographer's tendency to quickly dismiss, or at least neatly compartmentalize, the social scientist's concerns.

Social Scientist:
> I was thinking that the text excerpts were in a sequence…and the dance followed the sequence of the text. How does the choreographer select the sequencing? Do these six excerpts get repeated in different movements throughout the piece? How do the excerpts fit together? Is one more important than the others? We need to think about how this particular piece was inspired from one participant, not several. How do we convey this? Do we have to convey this?

---

[5] At this point, the social scientist was living and working in the UK. See Appendix E for more detail.

Choreographer:
> ...My initial response is no. This dance concert is not a "representation" of the data. It's symbolic of the data, but has no responsibility to accurately represent the data.

In the following exchange, the social scientist poses a question that allows the choreographer to locate a critical point concerning how discipline-specific training deeply affects collaborative research. The conversation below also exposes stereotypes at work in our own language and presumptions. Notice how we ally the concepts of intellect and prescriptive linearity with social science and meaning-making and personal response with the arts.

Social Scientist:
> Am I wanting a linear narrative and this interferes with me just "experiencing" the piece? Am I doing too much "intellectualizing" of the piece?

Choreographer:
> This is a great point to make about the challenges of transdisciplinarity. I'm very comfortable with abstract suggestion and varied meaning-making within my target audience. My guess is that is different for you as a social scientist.

These interactions gave the social scientist considerable pause. She had to reconsider her privileging of patterns and ask why she superimposed this expectation onto the choreographer. This led her to query the significance of patterns in her own work, particularly with regard to what might be left out in the process of looking for patterns. She asked: "How do patterns gloss over provocative data, incisive ideas? How do patterns fundamentally flatten the complexity of participants' lives? Are there other ways to engage with the data?"

As is illustrated, the social scientist raised (initial) concern that six of the aforementioned statements used as stimuli for one dance were all from one participant. This was troubling to the social scientist because there were 18 participants in the dataset. This plunged the social scientist into serious debate about representations and the ways in which she was trained to interact with data and think about the 'representation' potential from social science work. Did it matter that only one participant was included in the creation of the dance? Was the participant highly articulate and able to capture the 'essence' of several participants' experiences—or is this the 'wrong' question? At the end of the day, what can be represented? People? Experiences? Concepts? Feelings? Tropes? As Goffman and Lather remind all social scientists, true representation (i.e., one to one correspondence) is impossible.

Using both constructivist and critical framing paradigms the social scientist could accept that the choreographer engaged deeply with one participant and used the text excerpts that "struck" her. Although this was resolved, the social scientist then had nagging questions about the six text excerpts that the choreographer used. She was intrigued (and confused) by the choreographer's use of "The yellow roses were gorgeous." She worked hard to convince herself of the value of this data excerpt. In her reading of the data, she passed over this text excerpt (in her findings, it is subsumed in the desire and performance of perfectionism). The text excerpt itself was simply not that compelling to the social scientist.

The choreographer, though, interpreted "The yellow roses were gorgeous" as a bride's confirmation that her wedding had been "good." To the choreographer, that sentiment was ripe with kinesthetic potential. In the dance "I Was Happy in the Pictures," the motif built from this excerpt appears at the beginning and end of the dance as the soloist cuts through the stage, attempting to "make sure" that all aspects of her wedding day are in place, the way they "should" be. The choreographer did not anticipate a need to consider the source of the data excerpts because she was not concerned with re-presenting *patterns* or *participants*. She was concerned with kinesthetically re-presenting experiences and expressions that could *embody* the data in a meaningful and resonant way.

UNEXPECTED DATA

Although the social scientist experienced considerable discomfort with some of the "products" from the choreographer's engagement with the dataset, she also was encouraged to consider a broader conceptualization of data within a transdisciplinary project. As identified at the onset of this chapter, the social scientist initially remarked that she had little "audience data" from the third performance. This was presented to the choreographer as a huge disappointment. In response, the choreographer pointed out that the social scientist did indeed have "evidence"/data from the performance—as a dancer, the choreographer felt the audience members' responsiveness. They laughed at the appropriate times, they stayed for the entire performance, and they had supportive body language. According to the choreographer, the dancers themselves had data in their bodies as they performed and as they experienced the loud audience appreciation at the end of the performance. Not realizing how her disappointment and confusion about the lack of responsiveness through social science data collection could be interpreted as insulting to the choreographer and the dancers - as if their experiences of the performance didn't "count" as data or were not as valid as a survey or focus group would have been, the social scientist remained true to her training in wanting "measurable" feedback from the audience - data she could readily analyze!

Gradually, the social scientist began to realize how limited her scope of data had been and started considering alternative ways of documenting the audience's reactions (including having people in the audience gauging audience reactions, describing the affective atmosphere of the audience at the performance, foregrounding the dancers experience, etc.). The social scientist also realized that asking for focus groups immediately after the performances was not working—at the first two performances, only a few people stayed for the focus group and although the focus groups offered useful data, the social scientist had anticipated having more than one focus group at each performance (i.e., the response rate of 5 or 6 people from audiences of more than 100 people was surprising to the social scientist). It was only after the third performance with no one staying for a focus group that the social scientist opened up her thinking around data collection in the transdisciplinary project.

While working on *Ordinary Wars*, the social scientist had gone to a Paul Taylor Dance Company performance and stayed for the "talkback" session. The concept of a talkback session (essentially, the dancers/choreographers(s) and audiences dialoguing immediately after a concert) was new to the social scientist. It was after observing the talkback session and also dialoguing with her social science colleague Dr. Libby Balter Blume that the social scientist considered the possibility of having a "hybrid" focus group/talkback session at the end of the performances. She talked to the choreographer and they decided to try the combination: audience members could ask the dancers, choreographers, and researchers questions and the researchers could ask the audience members questions. This approach, which we used at the fourth and fifth performances, has proven much more successful and has provided us with a rich understanding of the ways in which audiences are responding to *Ordinary Wars*. Although we ended up in with a successful solution, getting there was fraught with discomfort and uneasiness. Recognizing the power of our discomfort and attempting to harness it, we delineate a methodology of discomfort in the next chapter.

CHAPTER 4

Toward a Methodology of Discomfort

"There is so much written descriptively about the content and form of such [transdisciplinary] research but very little critical thought focused on the theoretical, methodological and ethical challenges encountered by the scientists, artists and trainees engaged in conducting these projects" (Hodgins and Boydell 5).

Image 7: "I Was Happy in the Pictures," taken at March 2015 performance, Lubbock, Texas

HOW DO WE WORK (TOGETHER) IN OUR PROJECT?

It is fair to say that our working relationship has been bumpy. A few months into our project, the social scientist raised a critical question about our process of working together. She asked whether we were actually collaborating or simply working in parallel. The social scientist wondered if, due to the personal nature of choreography, it was possible for a kinesthetic analysis (resulting in the development of choreography) to be collaborative. Her concerns stemmed from feeling disassociated with the actual dance-making and from reading reviews of literature detailing performative social science events in which the original researchers "surrendered" (e.g., Bagley and Cancienne) their data to their partnering artists. The social scientist questioned whether we were unconsciously replicating that kind of partnership rather than actually working collaboratively (i.e., together) to re-analyze the data.

The choreographer, on the other hand, did not anticipate that the actual choreographic process would be a collaborative one, as the social scientist was not trained in dance composition. Instead, the choreographer wondered *how* the social scientist would be (or could be) a participant in the dance-making other than as a critical viewer and responder, which could reinforce a more parallel and less collaborative working relationship.

Concerns like these prompted us to question the philosophical frameworks and practical constraints of our collaboration and encouraged us to create a series of guiding questions (see Table 3) that we have pursued as vital not only to our own process but also to the larger, emerging enterprise of transdisciplinary collaboration. In a sense, these questions helped us figure out how to "do" transdisciplinary collaboration. What we have tried to do is ask these questions routinely in our work together. For example, in Chapter 3, we noted our discovery that we had, in one of our written exchanges, been reinforcing stereotypical descriptions of social science as logical and linear and of dance as interpretive and subjective. We were able to make that discovery by reflecting on the questions posed in Table 2, specifically questions of equity.

Table 2: Guiding Questions

Questions of Authority	How do we legitimately comment on each other's data analyses and ensuing findings/output?	What, if any, basic knowledge of each other's fields is necessary to effectively dialogue?	How can lack of knowledge increase awareness of individual practice/approach?
Questions of Parameters	What are the boundaries of collaboration?	When does critical engagement become disengaged?	What practices support and/or hinder mutual, sustained, and critical engagement?
Questions of Equity	In what ways does the nature of our project promote an equitable understanding of disciplines and approaches?	How can we participate in transdisciplinary collaboration without exploiting and/or privileging one field at the expense of the other(s)?	How can we be constantly mindful of disrupting stereotypical depictions of our fields?
Questions of Reciprocity	Is there an inherent conflict between the integrity of the data and the integrity of the dance?[1]	Will the data be a meaningful part of the final product?	In what ways can a transdisciplinary approach promote a process of symbiosis?

---

[1] There is precedent for this question in the existing literature. See Bagley and Cancienne.

The longevity of our collaboration has necessitated the development of practices that not only acknowledge but also actively engage with the questions presented in Table 2. In order to more closely examine these questions, we provide examples of how we worked with two types of questions from it.[2]

QUESTIONS OF AUTHORITY

We agreed very early on in our collaboration that neither one of us had expertise in the other's home discipline. What that meant was that we had to find ways to talk about each other's work (the social scientist's data and the choreographer's dances) that privileged the authority of the act of engaging (e.g., reading, viewing) over the authority of discipline-specific knowledge. For example, we elected to record the social scientist's reaction to viewing one of the dances for the very first time. We then published her reaction as a statement hung in the lobbies of the concert theatres in order to promote that her comments on the dance were legitimate and valuable in the context of our project, even though she does not have disciplinary "authority" in the subject. For the dance, "I Was Happy in the Pictures," she wrote:

> This was the first dance I viewed from the concert. I found it intense and moving. At first, I struggled with abstract movement as I kept trying to figure out what the choreographer wanted to convey to the audience. The tension and bewilderment conveyed in the dance was consistent with many of the participants' descriptions of weddings and their ensuing transition to being wives.

The realization that we could each offer valuable feedback to the other's area of expertise has afforded us the opportunity to stay engaged with each other and with the project in a very meaningful way. It has encouraged us to question the insulation that can come with seeking out or valuing only feedback that originates from colleagues within either discipline and uncovered unexpected questions and perspectives that led to greater reflection and consideration of choices. This commitment to "play down" our disciplinary paradigms in favor of questioning the unknown has been a major factor in sustained engagement.

We have not always been successful in that area, though, and have had to work through major moments in which our engagement with each other, and therefore the project, has been hindered. These moments largely boil down to issues with misunderstanding or not being aware of each other's disciplinary needs. Ultimately, the choreographer is not a social scientist, and the social scientist is not a choreographer. This is more complex than it might seem: dismissing the obvious indicates an inattention (deliberate or not) to the construct of disciplinary identity. Working in a transdisciplinary way means being willing to question standards of our disciplines. This is not only incredibly challenging from a practical perspective but can also be a real emotional blow. It can feel like

---

[2] Table 2 and the text preceding it were originally published by the authors in the *International Journal of Qualitative Methods* and are used here with permission.

a rejection and betrayal of what we know, thus on some level, of who we are. We have consequently termed this "disciplinary humility," and we promote it as a critical component of transdisciplinary work.

QUESTIONS OF EQUITY/QUESTIONS OF RECIPROCITY

What is generally publicized about collaborative endeavors is the *opportunity* associated with such projects, including the possibility for new and innovative products and the ways in which working with another person can augment a single researcher's profile. We argue that interested researchers should look to their tensions and conflicts as a source of critical discoveries. For example, through the conversation described in Chapter 3 that surrounded the dance "I Was Happy in the Pictures" (and others like it), we began to locate patterns of disciplinary "gripping" (i.e., clinging to our disciplinary training) in our work together. In order to get to a place of disciplinary humility, we had to first experience the gripping and then figure out why that was happening.

For context, the social scientist argues that qualitative research is already questioned in the larger field of social science (e.g., Gilgun; Morse et al). When the choreographer questioned the social scientist's values as a qualitative researcher (by questioning her choices concerning use of data), the social scientist (at times) responded defensively; she was operating from a position of disciplinary marginalization. Likewise, the choreographer is intimately aware of the ways in which dance is routinely questioned as a legitimate academic endeavor. More than once, she interpreted the social scientist's comments or critiques as attacks on her intelligence.

We were able to determine that our disciplinary gripping resulted from both of us reacting defensively to the other because of perceived threats to our disciplinary identities. Defensive posturing, as we term it, is not only counterproductive, it is also subversive. It operates without direct acknowledgment until the posturing manifests as a crisis. For example, early on, the social scientist was looking for more or less "accurate" accounts of the participants' stories to be re-presented in the dance performance. The social scientist's conditions were primarily based on *her* understanding of and interaction with the data (and her understanding of "data," in general, as discussed in Chapter 3). This did not map onto the choreographer's interpretation of the data, especially because she approached the data using entirely different, and disciplinary-specific, methodological practices.

The social scientist ended up setting a "bottom-line" standard of avoiding "inaccuracy" or "misrepresentations." The social scientist did not want the performance to "contradict" or be "in opposition to" the data from her initial datasets. She was comfortable with the choreographer's divergent readings of the data and believed this was to be expected but was uncomfortable when dances promoted a "wrong" interpretation of the research by audience members (as partially evidenced from the pilot audience data).

The choreographer became very frustrated with what she perceived as a real infringement not only on her artistic license but also on the ability of audience members to create their own interpretations of the choreographies. The choreographer did not fundamentally understand how the social scientist's requests were tied to the social scientist's disciplinary identity.

It is important to note that we are not the first collaborators to experience questions about disciplinary identity, integrity, and/or reciprocity. Boydell captures this issue particularly well, writing on arts-based approaches to health research:

> I faced this representational issue when using dance to share our research findings on pathways to care for young people experiencing psychosis. I questioned what might have been sacrificed for the sake of performance and the choreographer questioned what might have been sacrificed for the sake of the research. For example, would leaving the performance open to a greater level of interpretation result in a product that was less true to the research? Would too much of an emphasis on the research findings affect the artistic qualities of the dance? We arrived at a mutual agreement that it was essential to maintain the integrity of the key features of the data and hence the lived experience; however, the ways in which to do so were frequently ambiguous (Hodgins and Boydell 9).

Boydell's point concerning the ambiguity of procedures in transdisciplinary research is key. Often, in the absence of clear guidelines and when crisis mode has been reached, researchers will start to look for a way out. We suggest that the key here is not to search for a speedy resolution, but rather to reflexively question *why* the selected approaches or parameters are being used. In other words, how do they serve the project? This question effectively promotes disciplinary humility by positioning the project ahead of either researcher's discipline.

THE GOING GETS TOUGH

Frequently, our conflicts, like those described above, led to a general *working state* of discomfort. While our feelings of discomfort were not initially designed to expose or problematize restrictive discipline-specific practices, upon reflective analysis, both the social scientist and the choreographer identified major innovations in ways of making meaning that resulted from our discomfort with each other. This is a critical point: we argue that working in a state of discomfort holds incredible potential for transformative growth and change. In the following paragraphs, we offer an example from our working process as a practical lens through which to consider theoretical implications for a methodology of discomfort.

At the outset of our collaboration, the social scientist articulated to the choreographer the parameters of each study and, in discussions with the choreographer throughout the process, argued for the centrality of singlehood as a re-presented concept in the concert. The choreographer agreed with the social scientist fully on this point. During the process of actually making the concert, though, the choreographer became more concerned with artistic development of the dance works and the concert as a whole than with the saliency of singlehood.

It is noteworthy that the researchers were, at this point, acting in the best interests of their own disciplines, though that turned out to be counterproductive within a transdisciplinary structure.

A significant conflict developed when the choreographer disagreed with the social scientist about the design content of a specific dance[3]. The choreographer and the social scientist enjoyed the dance as a structurally important part of the concert, and the choreographer was not concerned with the artistic and design choices, specifically concerning costumes, music, and literal narrative. However, the social scientist was troubled by the potential she saw for viewers (prompted by the design elements) to interpret the dance in a way that contradicted the data on which the dance was based.

To clarify, when we began our project, the social scientist deliberately refrained from communicating her findings to the choreographer. She did share the design of the two studies, but she did not speak about her own analysis of either study. In fact, the social scientist was very careful even speaking generally about the data out of concern that she might unnecessarily narrow the choreographer's engagement with the datasets. As noted in Chapter 1, we were very interested in a collaboration in which the choreographer worked from the raw data rather than the social scientist's analysis of it. What the social scientist did not anticipate was that the choreographer would give so little attention to the social scientist's "essential elements" (i.e., parameters for being in the study).

The social scientist did not communicate how important to her these essential elements were because, for her, those elements were presumed. They constituted the foundational basis of and set the parameters for the studies. As the social scientist wrote to the choreographer, "I didn't communicate because I didn't think I had to…In my mind, the parameters of the study (i.e., being single, newly married) are the basis of the study. Thus, no need to remind anyone. It would be like reminding students to bring a notebook to class. It is so obvious you don't say it."

For the choreographer, though, those elements did not carry the same weight. The choreographer was focused on the expressions of the participants (documented in the transcripts). Though she understood the essential elements, she did not assign them the critical roles they occupied for the social scientist. What was exceedingly obvious for the social scientist was obscured for the choreographer and neither researcher realized the other's perspective until the conflict manifested as a sharp disagreement about, as previously mentioned, design choices.

At the height of this disagreement over design choices, the social scientist wrote a "clarity statement" to help her more fully express why she was unwilling to accept some of the choreographer's suggestions. The exercise of writing the statement was invaluable for her because it helped her come to terms with taken-for-granted disciplinary ties and voice her role and the role of social science in this project. The act of writing also gave the social scientist distance and perspective, and to some extent relieved her concerns that she needed to carry the

---

[3] This dance was one of the three choreographed by one of the two secondary choreographers.

weight of the integrity of social science on her shoulders. An excerpt from that statement reads:

> The standard that I feel I can have in a project like this is that I need to have some control that the performance <u>does not contradict the data.</u> Of course, I cannot control how the audience interprets abstract dance and, for the most part, I do not want to do so. I agree with you that the abstractness allows a multiplicity of interpretations and I think that is good—it is especially good to have feminist space for women to reflect on diversity of interpretations related to their identities. At the same time, I do want to make sure that the literal representations of the data (that is, titles, choreographers' statements, text, and images, songs with lyrics, etc.) and the data itself (text excerpts) are not being used in a way that clearly distorts the data.

The choreographer, particularly after reading the social scientist's clarity statement, understood the social scientist's perspective. Through reading the social scientist's detailed explanation of her approaches to data and the larger project, the choreographer began to understand that the social scientist was not critiquing the *artistic merit* of the dances, but was approaching the project in ways that made disciplinary sense to her. It is important to note that this was not a one-way street; after the choreographer read the social scientist's clarity statement, she began to consider her own tendencies to privilege her disciplinary practices and values.

However, for the choreographer, understanding the social scientist's clarity statement did not make the process of working, negotiating, or dialoguing *easier*. The choreographer understood what the social scientist was arguing, but fundamentally disagreed with her and was deeply wounded (this relates back to our contention that transdisciplinary work can threaten researchers' professional identities). She wrote, in response to the social scientist:

> You value different things than I value in this project. That is one of the reasons our work is truly groundbreaking. Our different values, though, cannot be placed in opposition to each other or in a hierarchical structure. There has to be room for me not to value the data (and the parameters of the data) the way that you do and for me to question its role. I will make room for you to value certain parts of the performance more or less than I do and question their inclusion. We have to legitimately support each other to move forward.

This was more than just a conflict crisis (a crisis centered on a specific disagreement); it was a philosophical crisis and identifies a crucial question: In developing transdisciplinary approaches to collaboration, must the collaborators *feel* good about their choices? In other words, can a transdisciplinary project be called a success (in that it meets the goals set forth at its conception) if its creators are not at ease with the choices they've made?

Theoretically, a researcher can disagree with or feel frustrated by a decision yet acknowledge that the decision is best for the process at hand because there is some clear indication of how the process *should* proceed. In transdisciplinary work, though, the process is not standardized; it is, rather, wholly dependent on the collaborators, their individual values, their shared goals and perspectives, etc. When the researchers are in crisis, the project is actually in crisis, too. To investigate this interdependence, we examine discomfort as a methodological practice in transdisciplinary collaboration.

Harnessing Discomfort

Discomfort has emerged as an effective methodological tool in our work together and we suggest that it is uniquely positioned as key to successful transdisciplinary work. Although the kinds of tensions from which discomfort stems will never be uniform across all transdisciplinary projects, we suggest that the *existence* of tensions is inherent in this kind of work, meaning that discomfort can be understood as a standard characteristic of transdisciplinary projects. We propose here a structure for *working within* discomfort in order to facilitate governable crises that might serve as catalysts for transformative, transdisciplinary (and possibly disciplinary) change and growth.

A first step is mapping the conflict. However, doing that is impossible until at least some conflicts have already happened; because transdisciplinary projects are so unique, it is difficult to accurately predict with any specificity the kinds of conflicts that will arise. Once conflicts have emerged and been identified, it is helpful to put them into a visual relationship with each other. This promotes three elements that are necessary to "harness" discomfort as a methodological tool for transdisciplinary research: awareness, acknowledgement, and identification of shared concerns.

Sometimes, one partner in a project might be unaware of the root of the other's discomfort even after a conflict. Making space for each researcher to consider *why* she is experiencing discomfort (*why* she is tense/frustrated/angry, etc.) promotes the idea that there is value in that root cause. Awareness, though, does not imply understanding or agreement. That's why we choose to use the term acknowledgement. Even in conflict, we can acknowledge each other's perspectives, thereby valuing them, without necessarily understanding or agreeing with them. Finally, creating a visual representation of discomfort promotes the identification of shared concerns. Where do our tensions overlap? We suggest a simple Venn diagram approach, as illustrated here, in Table 3:

Table 3: Venn diagram of discomfort

Social Scientist | Choreographer

Social Scientist:
- Categorization of the project
- **Control** of how data were presented
- Scientific **integrity**
- Is data "only" the original text and/or written responses to the concert
- Is the concert a **valid representation** of the data?
- Surrendering **data**

Choreographer:
- Choroegraphic/artistic **control** (commonly called license)
- Artistic **integrity**
- Amount of data
- Getting the analysis **"right"**
- Obligation to the **data**
- Is data the way the dancers/choreographers feel about the performance?

We start by listing the details of our discomfort. We visually illustrate how working in this state can, if the researchers are not careful, lead to each researcher feeling that her discomfort actually prevents her from finding common ground with her partner. We represent that isolation by leaving the overlapping area of the diagram above completely blank.

A second step in the mapping process is taking time to discuss each of these in turn. We recommend a discussion that draws on some of dance choreographer and educator Larry Lavender's points about engaging in critical feedback when responding to viewed choreography. In particular, Lavender recommends that responders avoid "high-inference" (72) language, or language that communicates a sense of value. Consider, for example, if the choreographer responded to the social scientist's discomfort with Categorization by stating, "Why would you ever be concerned with that? Obviously, we are not doing *just* social science." This is high-inference. This language communicates that the social scientist's concern has very little value. Instead, we recommend language that directly *acknowledges* each area of discomfort. Using the same example, the choreographer might respond, "I appreciate how important categorization is in your discipline and that you are concerned about professional ramifications if we "miscategorize" our project. I don't share your discomfort in this area, but I am open to hearing how you think we might move forward."

Finally, after each researcher has had the opportunity to discuss her discomforts and respond to her partner's, we recommend working together to identify any overlap. Using the diagram from Table 3, we focus in on that middle section, the "overlap," and identify our shared areas of discomfort:

Now, we are to a place of potential. Mapping our discomfort provides us with four shared concerns. Using this approach, researchers can assess tensions surrounding the identified, shared concerns purposefully, working to problematize their own practices in order to expose biases and boundaries in their disciplinary approaches. In the paragraphs below, we move briefly through each of these in order to illustrate our post-mapping dialogues, conversations that are critical to maintaining engagement with the process and product.

Control

A fundamental issue we consider in our project concerns ontological status. At one time or another, we have asked each other all of the following questions: What is reality and whose reality are we re-presenting? Whose reality is being danced: The choreographer's? The performers'? The social scientist's? The participants'? All of these simultaneously or none of these? Is it all merely fragments? What about realities being felt by audience members? How, if at all, are the viewers mapping onto their own realities in viewing the dances?

Because the social scientist and choreographer differently attend to and value these distinct realities, considerable tension emerged in the process leading to the presentation of our final concert. The social scientist and choreographer shared a working state of discomfort concerning the control over defining and setting the terms of reality(ies).

For example, after articulating the basic question of control of realities in this project, the social scientist began to ask questions about the extent to which she holds onto "ghost-like" figures in her research. She had to confront the fact that she only had fragments of the women's lives and the fragments she did get were under very narrow conditions (one interview, a set of guided questions, one day in time, etc.); social scientists argue that little is gained from a single interview (e.g., Skeggs). This line of questioning encouraged an awareness of social scientists' elusive goal of "representing" when representations *never* really represent the people involved (Goffman). This pushed the social scientist to consider whether she might move to a social science of evocation instead of representation (Koelsch).

Considering the "right" to control the terms of reality as a means of problematizing her own process, the choreographer began to question fundamental "realities" of dance-making, specifically concerning artistic license and the ethics of re-presentation. In trying to examine, for example, her reasons for wanting to keep a particular sound score, gesture or costume, the choreographer began to question her privileging of her own reality of interpretation (of the data) over the realities of the participants. The choreographer determined that a possible motive for this privileging might be rooted in coercing an expected audience response. This, in turn, acknowledges not only that the choreographer (for all of her insistence on divergent and subjective meaning-making) might be trying to elicit specific audience responses but also that this attempt could have actually benefitted the project if she had been able to communicate this to the social scientist at an early stage.

Integrity

As illustrated in Chapter 2 in our discussion on the complexities of categorization, the social scientist was initially operating with a set of expectations about the integrity of the project. Her expectations were based entirely on her knowledge of and projection toward how other social scientists would receive *Ordinary Wars*. The choreographer, as is also noted in Chapter 2, was concerned that fully accommodating all of the social scientist's requests would dilute the artistic integrity of the dances, something she dreaded when considering how other choreographers and dancers would respond to them.

An interesting example of a tension surrounding integrity in our collaboration comes from how we approached the original data. Whereas the social scientist generated meaning from the data by engaging in multiple readings and intense scrutiny of each transcript while also reading the wider literature and developing common themes from her readings and scrutiny, the choreographer generated meaning by using the data as a starting point. The choreographer's secondary analysis of the data, then, was not only significantly less comprehensive than the social scientist's primary analysis, it also (arguably) resulted in a series of dances that had more to do with the choreographer than with the data.

Ultimately, this is a question of integrity, but it is more complex than it might seem. By asking whether the choreographer's approach to the data preserved the integrity of a social science expectation for analyzing data (and also whether promoting the integrity of the concert required forsaking the integrity of the data, and vice versa) we also ended up asking how integrity in each of our disciplines is conceived and practiced. The social scientist, after significant reflection, acknowledges now that she felt hamstrung by the data, and concluded that trying to look for patterns across 35 participants left her with the unsettled feeling of severely flattening the complexity of the data itself. This, of course, raised more ethical and moral questions about her research engagements and her expectations for integrity as informed by her discipline.

The choreographer, for her part, moved to a position of aligning integrity, in a project like this, not with artistic preference or the original data, but rather with the process of collaboration. She advocates that other transdisciplinary collaborators identify the ways in which the process of working together both defines and maintains integrity as specific to the project in question. This affords a breadth to the concept of integrity that encourages researchers to value, but question, their disciplinary understandings of the term while simultaneously working together to understand integrity in the context of the project.

Data

Data, as described in more detail in Chapters 3 and 5, has been a recurrent source of discomfort and tension. For example, the social scientist experienced considerable angst when she learned about the development of two dances for the concert premiere that had not been shown in the pilot performance. This meant that the social scientist did not have audience data regarding viewers' interpretations of those dances. One of the new dances raised serious concerns for the social scientist as she surmised that audience members would map on to literal aspects of the dance (lyrics in the song, props, title of the song) and she perceived these as contradictory to the data.

After significant, and sometimes contentious conversation, the social scientist ended up asking herself whether she *could* know what was "oppositional" to the data, whether she was confusing data with her participants' social identities, and whether she was over-reliant on participants' and pilot data (i.e., could she not make decisions outside of having data, even in a project like this?). As one artist asked her at a scholarly presentation: How would it even be possible for the dances to "misrepresent the data"?

The choreographer, conversely, was not guided by a need to "accurately" represent the data. Unlike the social scientist, the choreographer was not particularly concerned with the possibility that audience members might interpret portions of the concert in ways that "contradicted" the data [4]. For the choreographer, the (seemingly) constant need to "back up" her choices with audience data was exhausting, until she began to consider that the social scientist was not fundamentally trying to gauge the "accuracy" of her dances, but rather to find out what audience members were seeing in the dances and investigate how those perceptions connected, if at all, to the original data. This shift in thinking allowed the choreographer to more fully understand the importance of the social scientist's relationship to the original data and to question whether relationship to the data should be a key component of shared grounding (see "Moving Forward," below).

---

[4] This highlights a "productive incompatibility" between dance and social science: in dance choreography and performance, constructs of "right" and "wrong" (with exceptions made for technical execution of some choreographed movement) are *subjective*.

Getting it "Right"

The question of "misrepresentation" is also at the heart of what we discovered was another shared area of discomfort: a sincere concern with "rightness." Another way to think about this is to articulate the concept of rightness as an ethical responsibility to the original data and to the individuals who provided that data. The idea of getting it "right" both transcended and relied on our disciplinary approaches to the project. For example, although we each had trepidation about producing something that might "betray" the original participants, that concern manifested for the social scientist as a concern about "accurate" re-presentation of the participants and for the choreographer as a concern about disparaging the participants or their experiences.

Interestingly, it seems that our audiences are also concerned with "rightness." Routinely, we are asked whether the original participants in the social scientist's research have seen the concert.[5] There is a keen interest, we find, in whether the original participants might confirm that their stories are "correctly" re-presented onstage. The choreographer would suggest that this interest illustrates not only a preoccupation with "rightness" but also with the notion that there is a "most correct" way to interpret the dances.

MOVING FORWARD

What we've discovered over the course of our four-year collaboration, is that much of what we advocate could not have been predicted or planned. It depended wholly on the discomfort in the doing. In discussing ways in which researchers might use discomfort as a methodological tool, we do not intend to prescribe a tidy set of procedures that will result in a "successful" collaboration. The substance of transdisciplinary research is, as we've argued, its messiness. That does not mean, though, that there cannot be overarching guidelines for transdisciplinary researchers that offer collaborators a basic framework for a working process. In addition to recommending that a part of that framework include the use of discomfort as a research tool, we present three additional structural guides for collaborators to consider: duo-memoing, relationship analysis, and shared grounding.

Duo-memoing

Keeping our commitment to exposing the messiness of the project and analyzing our process of working together, we engaged in extensive reflection. What is relatively unique about our reflection practices is that we engaged in *dual-reflection*—attempting to capture our engagement with each other and pushing

---

[5] This is an important question, and we always appreciate people asking it. The social scientist has not invited the original participants to the live concert because of the financial and practical implications associated with doing so. Instead, the social scientist and the choreographer are working to create an online viewing experience and a post-viewing focus group/talkback to which we might invite all of the original participants.

each other's reflections in real-time. Through working on this project, we developed a term, duo-memoing, to capture our processes. In qualitative research, many scholars practice "memoing," that is, continuously posing analytical and theoretical considerations and questions about decisions made in the research process. Extending this, duo-memoing involves a *joint* process of continuous questioning that is dependent on a collaborative (rather than individual) approach.

We engaged in duo-memoing primarily through our extensive, audio-recorded discussions. We have more than 100 hours of audio-recordings and many pages of transcriptions documenting our conversations. The audio recordings and transcripts provide us with the ability to re-visit our decisions, our shifting language and discourses (including professional jargon use), as well as our emotional expressions. Following is an example of the choreographer writing to the social scientist explicitly about *how* duo-memoing encouraged growth and transformation:

> I think that our low points have...resulted in some of our most groundbreaking and inspiring moments. Part of this is because when we feel like we have to explain our perspectives to each other in detailed writing, we end up exposing our own patterns, preferences, and (for lack of a better word) biases. This process of self-discovery has been one of the very best things about working on this project. I do not know that I'd have made these discoveries otherwise.

Systematically and repeatedly reflecting on our process together is an innovative strategy for transdisciplinary collaboration—but is not limited to transdisciplinary projects. We encourage all scholars, practitioners, and instructors to consider the utility of duo-memoing as an effective and meaningful model of meta-analysis.

Relationship to the Project and its Parts

Very little will destroy a collaboration more quickly than an undiagnosed difference in each researcher's relationship to the project and/or its comprising parts. As mentioned earlier in this chapter, the social scientist had a defined relationship with the original data prior to embarking on this project with the choreographer. The choreographer not only lacked this relationship entirely, she had no way of predicting how that lack would affect the way the social scientist would engage with the project as a whole.

We recommend that if the researchers do not "start from scratch," that is, if one or the other has already begun work on some part of the project, they use the following questions to analyze the development of relationships to parts of the project and then discuss how the responses will factor into the transdisciplinary process of working:
- What is the scope of the work already completed? Some considerations here are the duration of the work, the researcher's relationship with it, and the methodology(ies).
- How, if at all, will the project use existing data (including lived experiences that are key components of the project)?

- In what ways, if at all, is the concept of ownership factoring into the completed work?

After the questions above have been answered, collaborators can then move to an explicit discussion of value connected to the identified relationships: more specifically, *why* is the data/experience/story important and *what* expectations does each researcher have for the ways in which the data/experience/story might be used in the project?

Shared Grounding

As mentioned in Chapter 1, the authors came to this project with a shared grounding in feminism. We strongly recommend that other potential transdisciplinary collaborators consider their shared groundings in order to be able to return to those places when the collaboration seizes. The critical nature of shared grounding in transdisciplinary projects has much to do with the value that the researchers assign that place (or those places) of grounding. In our case, when the research process became extremely difficult due to major conflicts and sharp tensions, a shared commitment to feminism provided us with something (*one* thing, it felt like, at times) in common.

Some key tenets of feminism, like reflexivity, analyzing taken-for-granted practices, questioning power and privilege, and allowing for discomfort emerged as touchstones in our process. In times of duress, we returned to these places because they are so valuable to each of us as ways of knowing and doing. Allowing for discomfort, in particular, was very challenging. However, we understood discomfort not only as a methodological tool for our own project but also as a feminist stance against giving in or resigning. Using discomfort productively encourages researchers to work against the idea that collaboration is about persuasion and acquiescence. More broadly, encouraging discomfort in the context of disciplinary training means that we are committed to exploring and critiquing our disciplinary practices and the ways in which, if at all, they function to maintain oppressive practices. That kind of commitment is key to a feminist approach to research; focusing in on that shared grounding in feminism allowed us to find a way back into the process when the challenges of working in a transdisciplinary way threatened to pull us completely apart.

CHAPTER 5

Crisis of Legitimation Magnified

Image 8: Dialogue between "Dressed" Parts 1 and 2, taken at March 2015 performance, Lubbock, Texas

LEGITIMACY[1]

We especially drew on our shared feminist theoretical commitments when responding to one of the greatest threats *inherent* in transdisciplinary projects—the crisis of legitimation. Arguably, legitimacy is the root of layered and sustained discomfort. We now turn to a focused discussion of the crisis of legitimacy and our responses to it.

Both qualitative and dance scholars in the academy are intimately familiar with the (on-going) challenges of legitimation (Denzin & Lincoln). We offer here that transdisciplinary projects magnify the crisis, primarily because of the issues

---

[1] The subsection "Legitimacy" was originally published by the authors in the *Journal of Family Theory & Review* and is used here with permission.

discussed in Chapter 2. In that chapter, we queried the role of disciplinary expertise in transdisciplinary collaborations. We further that discussion here with an eye toward transdisciplinary collaborations that include the arts as one or more of the participating disciplines.

We focus on the importance of disciplinary training respective to artists because of what we perceive as a considerable negligence and/or unawareness in this area, even on the part of individuals analyzing the larger concept and value of arts-based research. For example, writing on arts-based research, professor of art education David Pariser suggests that artists making art may change their minds on a "whim" with no expectation to vet said change through any external reviewing body (12).

A first flaw in Pariser's line of reasoning is this: using the word whim to describe an artist's decision to make a practical shift reinforces the common and tired understanding in the academy that artists are illegitimate researchers. Pariser's claim conflates artistic methods with arts-based research. When working independently on a new dance, a choreographer, and certainly the choreographer co-writing this book, may decide to change the direction of that dance based on her analysis of the work in progress. Pariser is correct that the choreographer does not vet that decision with the venue that will eventually produce her work or, generally speaking, with the dancers dancing it. However, the choreographer would not make the same, wholly independent decision when working collaboratively on an arts-based research project.

A more troubling flaw, though, is that Pariser contextualizes this statement within his larger argument that arts-based research (particularly as conceived by Eisner) is at heart an attempt from within the academy to legitimize the arts (2). This argument does not acknowledge the way in which the term "research" is deliberately constructed to align with and promote a certain way of knowing and doing (usually associated with the physical sciences). Further, there is no consideration given to the ways that the concept of research is publicized in the academy, particularly concerning tenure and promotion. Suggesting that a faction of the academy is using arts-based research as a means of legitimizing the arts rather than as a means of questioning the nature of the academy's construct of research furthers the idea that the arts are marginally important precisely because they do not, on their own, meet the requirements of being "research."

Pariser concludes that labeling arts practices "research" muddies over the differences between arts practices and science practices. That may be, but to suggest, as he does, that a scientific approach to research is "certainly more credible" than an "artistic approach that unashamedly privileges the creator's point of view" (13) pokes not one, but two, large elephants in the room: first, who gets to decide what is "credible" and when, and second, does scientific research not privilege the researcher's point of view? We focus below on the first elephant, and direct the reader to the discussion of control in Chapter 4 for more on the second.

The question of credibility returns to what Barone and Eisner bring forward when they encourage us to think about *why* we ally the term research with the kind of research largely used and valued most by the physical sciences (2). Why is a scientific approach to research more credible, per Pariser, than an artistic approach? This question, and others like it, point to an opportunity to evaluate how, in the academy, we are trained to privilege the standards of a certain set of disciplines as being more valuable, valid, or credible than any other. Instead of simply accepting that scientific research is the most legitimate form, we must consider that research, more broadly defined, does not and cannot have a singular goal. Thus, suggesting that one goal is better or more worthy than another communicates to *all* researchers a clear hierarchy of disciplines, practices, and values that appear to be endorsed by the academy.

Rumbold, Fenner, and Brophy-Dixon, writing on representation in arts-based research, guide readers to consider the inherently multi-purposed nature of research when they point to the ways in which what they term art-based research facilitates transformative, cultural (community) change (68). Certainly, this goal is as valuable as that of a more "scientific" approach to research that promotes verification of claims.

We offer this review in order to discard the idea that transdisciplinary research involving artists is not legitimate research. That stated, we now move on to a second argument for more attention to substantiating the legitimacy of transdisciplinary research involving the arts by advocating, as previously mentioned, for the essential inclusion of a trained artist.

The Dangers of "Rummaging"

It is encouraging to consider artistic expression and performance as interesting and engaging means of asking questions (researching). In Leavy's *Method Meets Art: Arts-Based Research Practice*, author and dancer Celeste Snowber acknowledges that "[the] transcendent and consciousness-raising capacities of dance can be harnessed by qualitative researchers to build methods and practices congruent with research related purposes" (181). However, we strongly caution against what much of the related literature reveals as commonplace: social scientists "borrowing" from the arts without collaborating with trained artists (Piercy and Benson; Arditti et al; Gergen and Gergen, *Playing*).

For example, for the duration of our collaboration, the artist and social scientist have written together. This is unique from nearly all of the writing/publications we have examined. Within performative social science literature, for example, the social scientist tends to be the sole author or shares authorship with another social scientist. To this point, the *International Review of Qualitative Research* journal recently published a special issue on "the Arts and Qualitative inquiry" (Summer 2014, volume 7). Of the eight articles in the journal, only one was written with/by artists. The rest were authored by social scientists, primarily in the field of education. The relative lack of additional literature featuring collaborating artists as authors raises the question of social scientists "rummaging" through the arts for promotional purposes and/or dissemination of findings. We have also encountered a tendency to "rummage" through the arts in other ways.

In their recent book, *Playing With Purpose,* Gergen and Gergen argue that "...social scientists doing performance do not have to be high-class performers to engage in this craft. The purpose [of performative social science] is different from what it would be if one set out only to 'entertain' an audience with a highly skilled rendition" (219). We find this sentiment problematic for several reasons, the most critical being that it belies an underlying assumption that artistic skill is somehow negligible in performative social science projects. Additionally, performative social science projects that aim to integrate social science and the arts but fail to involve or feature trained artists relegate performance, as a discipline, to a subordinate place in the collaboration. Dance, along with some other art forms, is already critically marginalized academically and culturally in North America. Researchers who use arts-based practices without actually working with artists affirm this marginalization, which we assert is a dangerous thing to communicate to audiences who view these projects.

Further, even if there is some substance to the claim that the *purpose* of performative social science is not to "'entertain' an audience with a highly skilled rendition," collaborators in performative social science projects are not absolved of working to maintain the integrity of performance. This argument is clearly echoed by dancers and dance educators who have been audience to projects that arguably trivialized the dance components. Quoted in *Dancing the Data* (Bagley and Cancienne), a dance educator provided the following feedback to a viewed project:

> One of the problems we have had in the dance world is being trivialized and the assumption that you can throw together a dance in two days or two minutes is very problematic. Watching it last night I thought this is so stereotypical, what are these people doing, it trivializes the art form and doesn't speak well for the dance profession (4).

In his essay on interventionist theatre as a learning medium, Tony Jackson argues that working toward disciplinary expertise *within* arts and education collaborations is not inherently contradictive, but inherently critical. He writes:

> My argument will attempt to push the boat out just a little further: to propose that, at its best, theatre that aims to educate or influence can *only* truly do so if it values entertainment, the artistry, and craftsmanship [sic] that are associated with resonant, powerful theatre, and the aesthetic qualities that—by definition—will appeal to our senses....Lose sight of the aesthetic, and the *capacity* of such theatre to intervene is seriously diminished (106).

Barone and Eisner echo this sentiment and propose that arts-based research reaches its fullest potential when the product (whatever that might be) can be viewed and evaluated as a work of art (1). That achievement, the choreographer would argue, wholly depends, at least in transdisciplinary projects, on the artist being *trained* in her discipline. We would caution here that advocating for disciplinary expertise (or training) in transdisciplinary projects does not stipulate the maintenance of disciplinary boundaries and/or the evaluation of the project according to disciplinary expectations. Rather, pushing for disciplinary expertise reminds the researchers that the quality of both the process and the product in transdisciplinary projects depends on the ability of the researchers to simultaneously use and question their disciplinary training. We cannot do this if we are not, to begin with, trained.

EVALUATION

As we began to mold what would become the *Ordinary Wars* concert, we started to consider how it would be assessed. Interestingly, our emphasis on disciplinary training served us well in looking toward how our project might be evaluated. As Barone and Eisner confirm, to be "useful, a piece of arts based research must succeed both as a work of art and as a work of research. It must be, that is, of sufficiently high quality to lead members of an audience into a powerful experience, into a researching of social phenomena" (145).

In dance, there is not a uniform set of standards against which all performance and choreography may be evaluated. The same is true for social science. In both cases, the genres of work produced within the disciplines are too varied to allow for the use of a single set of standards that enable a reviewer to make a judgment about the quality of a work. Further, promoting a single set of standards with which to evaluate dance performance or social science research privileges the standards over the work being reviewed, something that we oppose. Discouraging the use of standards, though, does not preclude encouraging the use of criteria.

Barone and Eisner go so far as to introduce a set of criteria for arts based research in general. That set includes the following elements: incisiveness, concision, coherence, generativity, social significance, evocation and illumination (148). We do not disagree that any of these are valuable criteria for arts based research products. However, we would suggest that transdisciplinary researchers consider an even more reflective approach. In transdisciplinary projects, the collaborators should work to develop a set of criteria (for evaluation of the eventual product of the research) that directly relates to their original or modified objectives. In our case, our overarching goal for our project remained stable. We aim to "affect change in our respective fields and in our communities by re-presenting, in an evening-length concert, data of women's experiences in "ordinary" conditions." That goal can be translated into a set of criteria directly related to its various components:

- Awareness
- Resonance
- Reflection
- Action

In the following section, we explore an overview of each criterion and then return to a discussion of how disciplinary training is critical to their effectiveness as a set.

Awareness

As briefly described in our introduction, we came to this project with a concern about the lack of ways in which women's "ordinary" decisions about their relational and reproductive lives were publicized in our own disciplines. A primary goal of the project was to simply raise awareness of how *un*ordinary these kinds of decisions (e.g., getting married, considering having children) are and how an overwhelmingly prescriptive social narrative precludes the ability of women to publicly question their relational and reproductive decisions.

To succeed, then, our project needed to make our audiences *aware* of the ways in which women are subject to narrowly defined constructs of marriage and motherhood. We were able to evaluate this criterion of awareness by asking our audiences to complete post-concert surveys and participate in post-concert talkback sessions. We identified specific questions to gauge audience awareness, for example (from the post-concert written survey): "What is your interpretation of tonight's concert as a whole? [You could describe images, themes, narrative ideas, emotions, or other responses.]" Some of the responses that we've received include the following statements. We've underlined the excerpts that, from our review, indicate awareness:

> "It was amazing to hear how different women have different opinions on marriage."

> "It was funny but also not funny—the parody was of true feelings and issues about being trapped in this normative cycle."

> "Great mind opener! As an activist feminist, I don't feel like I have a place in marriage, but even the government is trying to get me to marry."

> "Women are held down by society's expectations of how they are supposed to act."

> "I felt it was a correct representation on how society pressures women into marriage and having a family and anything else that deviates from that is abnormal and shameful."

> "Women are often pushed that there is only one way to conduct their life."

> "I enjoyed the performances, over all interesting to see both sides, the single and the married or those about to get married."

> "The struggle between societal norms and pressures on women to become "married" and the need to know and be an authentic self."

"It was very great and made me realize it's not just about the pretty, fancy-ring wedding, it's about everything that comes after."

Resonance

Resonance, a second criterion that we use to evaluate our project, cannot happen without awareness, though it is not guaranteed to follow. Resonance reflects reverberation in audience members' lives, thoughts, and emotions. Often, resonance is rendered intelligible through the sensory experience viewers describe. Resonance can be positive, but also deeply painful, or rooted in anger, fear, or frustration. The following statements, specifically the underlined segments, from our post-concert surveys illustrate the concept of resonance:

"I felt a feeling of guilt, in a way…of my own station."

"Love it. Very emotional for me as a single woman who has expressed a lot of the doubts about marriage."

"…So to me it was very powerful to hear and know I'm not the only one and that it's ok if I don't want kids."

"Positive and pleasurable. I laughed, connected, had an emotional response with the performance on different levels."

"Touched me, brought at my own emotions about the struggle of being single and being judged provoked a lot of emotion for me."

" 'Brave' makes me cry, y'all. As a lesbian, I felt both moved and also a teensy bit underrepresented, but, like, I get it."

Reflection

Reflection is an increasingly important part of our own research process. In order for our work to function as an instigator of transformative cultural change, it must encourage the viewer to reflect on the ways in which the issues presented on stage interface with the viewer's own lived experiences.

Maxine Greene might frame our concept of reflection as a way of being "wide-awake." In the clearest sense, it requires the viewer to move from awareness, through resonance, and then into a space of deliberately making personal connections. These kinds of connections are described in the comments of some of our viewers, with the underlined sections specifically illustrating reflection:

"I really loved the concert. I think it portrays ideas that aren't normally discussed, it lets me think about different ideas opposite to how I was raised."

> "As a whole I don't really know how to interpret it. Coming from a divorced family, my father failing twice at it and being predominately raised by my mother, my thoughts on women and the need to get married have always been that it is not supposed to be happy."
>
> "I felt like I could relate for my mother raising me to be a housewife because of my culture."
>
> "I loved the performance. My family has always been supportive of my choices, but there has been an underlying theme of traditional expectation."
>
> "I'm 35—I, too, have thought I better get after having babies, time's almost up/what's wrong with me?"
>
> "I've found myself thinking and even saying some of the things from the text."
>
> "This concert was really relatable to my current experiences."
>
> "From a male perspective, very illuminating. Many common issues that bear discussion as a culture."
>
> "Very similar to what we are going through as a soon to be married couple. Almost every bit of dialogue in the performance have been observed by my fiancé in the previous few months."

Action

Of all of our identified criteria, action is perhaps the most difficult because it requires either speculation or a secondary assessment. By action, we mean things that our viewers tell us they are going to do or things that our viewers report they have done after seeing *Ordinary Wars*.

In her book *Critical Pedagogy: Notes from the Real World*, Joan Wink describes action as a part of the cycle of critical pedagogy: to name, to critically reflect, to act. We follow Wink's lead here and consider that, as valuable as reflection is, reflection in and of itself does not engender transformative cultural change. That happens with action. Now, we're realistic about this. We don't expect immediate actions that create enormous impact craters. What we encourage, instead, are actions that lead to further awareness, further reflection, and ultimately, broader and more sustained action. Some examples of statements that suggest the potential for action follow:

> "I feel an immediate desire to discuss this with women I am close to like my sister, mother, and girlfriends. And any men willing to discuss topics explored."

"My favorite dance was "To Find My Voice." It made me realize that I can have all of the things that I want, regardless of what they are if I find my voice to say all that I want."

"Can y'all do another series like this including more topics like this? Maybe include homosexuality?"

"I wish I knew how to get involved with the project."

FOUR STARS

It is important to restate that in order to lead audiences to awareness, resonance, reflection, and action, the work must be of sufficiently high quality. It is precisely that attention to disciplinary quality that also allows the work to be reviewed by trained experts in the disciplines represented. Unlike standards used to evaluate, for example, the submission of a written work to an established journal, there is not a set of generally understood standards with which to evaluate transdisciplinary projects like ours. Because of that, our project cannot be compared to/judged against/accepted over other transdisciplinary projects for inclusion in some canon of "four star" collaborations. However, that should not discourage us, or other researchers, from seeking out or submitting our work for peer review and/or other evaluation.

It is legitimate, we argue, to provide a dance or social scientist reviewer who attends our concert with our list of criteria for evaluation. Our reviewer, then, can respond with an informed subjectivity (rooted in disciplinary expertise) to each of the identified areas. This approach reinforces the idea that success, as measured in transdisciplinary work, should be defined by the alignment of the work with its overarching goals as set forth by the researchers; as previously explained, disciplinary excellence is a critical part of that alignment. We have essentially removed the "venue" (journal, theatre, juried competition) from the equation: our success depends now on our ability to live up to our own expectations.

This is where we encounter the raised eyebrows. There is some suspicion, at least in academia, about work that is not peer reviewed by an agency defined by the discipline rather than the researchers. Katherine Boydell, a social scientist working with an artist on a collaborative project using an arts-based research approach, directly addresses this suspicion. She writes about her "...concern to remain 'legitimate' within the field of medicine, to do so means to fall back upon the common academic currency—peer reviewed publications and scientific presentations" (Hodgins and Boydell 5).

Our argument is this: we are not absolved of considering established standards and criteria for excellence in our home disciplines. If anything, our product demands an even greater attention to those elements, an attention that would be impossible if either of us lacked disciplinary expertise. In sum, because our product was created with an awareness of and an ability to meet expectations for quality work in dance and in social science, it can be reviewed by trained dance artists/critics and trained social scientists who *may* choose to comment on the discipline-specific components of the product, but who will, first and foremost, focus their review on the criteria we have identified as critical to our *transdisciplinary* success. In other words, our suggestion for project-based criteria for evaluation does not disqualify our project from being evaluated as social science or as dance, but requests, in a sense, that it be evaluated on a set of things that are not tied to either discipline, but to the aims of the project itself.

We include here peer reviews written by a dancer/choreographer and a social scientist; both attended an *Ordinary Wars* concert prior to the development of our identified criteria for evaluation. We encourage readers to consider how the work is received according to the expectations affiliated with its participant disciplines as expressed through the peer reviews. We further encourage readers to question what each review leaves out; that is, how are reviews that speak exclusively to one discipline or the other essentially incomplete?

Remarks from Rachel Ure, Dancer and Choreographer

I found *Ordinary Wars* to be a very enjoyable, enriching, and intimate experience. As a dancer, I appreciated the skill and sophistication found in choreography that was also very accessible for the audience. The variety of pieces along with well-utilized props and costumes kept me ever engaged and entertained. Each piece utilized the range of talent and life experience of the performers, making a small cast fill the show to brimming.

Durham DeCesaro's ability to speak volumes with simple gestures and display clear messages through intricate choreography is stunning. Her carefully chosen group of choreographers created pieces that supported one another while varying in style and weight. I loved that the wildly satirical " The Cowboy, The Lawyer, and the Stork" could then be followed by the beautifully haunting and abstract "To Find My Voice;" we, the audience, felt informed rather than jolted by the shift. The scripting and dance flowed well together - each one hinting to and adding depth to the other while letting the audience fill in some of the connections themselves.

"A Thin Line", choreographed by Ali Duffy, particularly spoke to me. I felt that her depiction of a woman balancing all that is expected of her, all that she desires to be, all that is on her plate was breath taking. The act of literally balancing on that line - at times falling off just to get back up and fight for balance - felt so universal to all people, but especially to women. Duffy's choice of staging and lighting created a feeling that I was looking on a very private struggle that is often unseen on the outside, but is very real.

Durham DeCesaro's choreographic artistry was beautifully depicted in "To Find My Voice." I loved watching the dancers move from unison movement into their own timing and facing of that same movement. In this way and others, the choreography skillfully captured the tension between being molded by others ideas of who we should be, and truly breaking free and finding our own voices. I felt the struggle of each dancer - each woman - as they were molded and closed by others, and then broke free with large arm gestures and unbound spacing. This piece set us up for a strong and empowering show ending.

In the intimate black box setting that I first viewed the show, I felt a strong connection to both the monologues and dance, even though I found that my own experience and feelings often differed from those being offered. It was the celebration and presentation of women's ideas, feelings, and desires that I connected with. I realized, sitting in the audience, just how important it is for voices and ideas to be shared in artful and compelling ways such as *Ordinary Wars*. I came away very satisfied with the dance content and thrilled at how the research, scripting and overall construction of the show drew me in and kept me thinking well after the show ended.

Remarks from Thomas W. Blume, Social Scientist[2]

I have been fascinated, in my clinical and scholarly lives as well as in my personal life, by the intersecting themes of transition and influence. When I began to see these themes I was working with adolescents; over the years I have come to believe that life is a constant process of experiencing pushes and pulls, balancing the calls for change with the sense of loss as we go into new places in our lives and leave old places behind.

As I watched the *Ordinary Wars* performance I was impressed with the dramatic way the dancers were able to embody the influence theme — voiced in their quotations from the research data—to show the tension between wanting to conform and yet feeling that one is "going through the motions." Their multiple enactments of the same cultural scripts were frighteningly similar. The frightening aspect, of course, was emphasized by the quotations from women who articulated the pushes and pulls that were leading them to make choices.

Those who would follow the marriage script and the wife/mother script were taking on new identities that felt somehow alien. They seemed to be kicking and silently screaming as they were being forced to accept these choices. Their tightrope walk expressed both fear that they

---

[2] Dr. Blume's full title follows: Thomas W. Blume, Ph.D., LMFT, LPC, Associate Professor and Coordinator, Couple and Family Counseling Specialization, Department of Counseling, Oakland University, Rochester, Michigan, USA, 48309. Author, *Becoming a Family Counselor: A Bridge to Family Therapy Theory and Practice*. Personal website: www.identityrenegotiation.com

wouldn't be able to perform and also the acceptance of the idea that once they started across the rope they would have to keep moving forward.

Those who saw themselves rejecting the dominant definitions of womanhood, on the other hand, were seeing both the joys of being authors of the own scripts and the fear that their individuality would be denied by those who would label them as failures and lump them together in a category that was not valued.

As I reflect on the performance, I wish I could share the performance with various audiences. I want other men to see it, hoping that the nonverbal messages might get through to them if they are not hearing the voices of the women in their lives. I want young women to see it, hoping that they would grow in self-love and self-acceptance through seeing this dramatic enactment of the shared themes in their individual struggles to choose among painful alternatives. And I want the parents, siblings, other relatives, and friends of these young women to see themselves sitting in the judges' chairs, hoping that they would find ways to step out of the influence process and connect with the feelings they have seen dramatized on stage.

As these two excerpts and the wider audience comments shared earlier in this chapter showcase, audience members tended to be highly engaged with the performance and they found the performance provocative. In the next chapter, we share how we collected the data, including our challenges, the modifications we made over time with data collection, and our shifting understandings of the data itself.

CHAPTER 6

Audience Data Collection

Image 9: "Dressed (Part 1)," taken at April 2015 performance, Lubbock, Texas

Over the course of our project, we have sought audience data from each of our performances, starting with the pilot performance. We have tried a variety of data collection methods, including paper and online surveys, text messaging between dances at the live performance, focus groups, and hybrid focus group/talkback sessions. The methods garnering the greatest success (i.e., receiving responses from the most audience members) were brief paper surveys (accompanied by payment) and the hybrid focus group/talkback sessions.

The last two performances yielded 45 paper surveys (out of an audience of approximately 100 people) and 100 paper surveys (out of an audience of 140 people); this was a considerable improvement over the rate of return for the online surveys (a total of 10 for three performances, with more than 300 audience members combined) and the longer written surveys. Additionally, we had between 20 and 45 people at each of the hybrid focus groups/talkback sessions at our last two performances. Prior to that, we had six people participating in the focus group at the first performance, seven at the second performance, and none at the third performance.

September 2012 Pilot Performance

In September 2012, we staged a pilot performance and asked audience members to provide feedback about what they saw. The pilot performance consisted of a long (approximately 10 minutes) opening dialogue and four dances. The performance lasted one hour. The audience comprised students who were required to attend the performance as a requirement for their undergraduate dance classes, their graduate sex/gender classes, or their graduate qualitative methods classes. Forty-four participants attended the pilot and all of them offered feedback.

Audience members were given a survey and a program when they arrived at the dance performance. Following IRB protocol, we asked them if they were willing to participate in the study, informed them of the purpose of the survey, and noted that their participation was voluntary and that they could stop the survey at any time. A third of the audience received a program with detailed text about the social science analysis of the studies as well as information about the titles of the dances, the choreographers, and the dancers (we called this Program A). Another third of the audience received a program with brief descriptions about the social science data and brief descriptions about the dances (we called this Program B). The final third of the audience received a program with only the title of the dances, the names of the choreographers, and the names of the performers. This is more aligned with a typical program for a dance concert and we called this Program C (see Appendix D for Programs). The distribution of the programs was random. The social scientist was interested in learning whether the level of detail hindered or supported audience members' interpretation of and engagement with the dances.

Participants were asked to respond to a series of questions (see Appendix A). The social scientist and choreographer separately read the audience members' comments and then discussed their reactions to the comments. The social scientist documented the differences among participants' responses based on which program they were given. She discovered that participants were more able to engage with and have a broader interpretation of the dances when they were provided with fewer details in the program. It was as if greater detail was more hindering for the participants, narrowing their interpretations. Because of this, the social scientist and choreographer decided to use the least detailed program for the final concert. In the lobby, we offered detailed information about the research and the process of creating the dances so that audience members would still have access to that information if interested.

From the data collected at the pilot, it was clear that the title of one of the dances, "Pregnant with Doubt," was problematic. According to the audience data, the title led participants to a literal interpretation of the dance, assuming the dancers were pregnant. None of the participants in the study from which the dance was developed were pregnant and the choreographer (in this case, one of the two secondary choreographers) had not intended for the audience to assume that the dancers were pregnant. Upon reading the data, the dance's choreographer (in agreement with the lead choreographer and social scientist) decided to retitle the dance "With Doubt." Audience data collected at the concert premiere and at subsequent performances indicated that the title change was effective, as very few audience members interpreted that the dancers in this work are supposed to be pregnant.

Other substantial modifications made to the concert as a direct result of the feedback from the pilot performance were to shorten the opening dialogue, use dialogue in between each dance, and include dialogue from the single women. The dialogue used in the pilot performance was only from the wedding study. As a result, most of the pilot audience members assumed that all of dances were about married women; the audience members were interpreting all of the dances as being directly connected to the opening dialogue. Single women were effectively rendered invisible, mapping onto the larger dialogue of singlehood (DePaulo and Morris; Sharp and Ganong). The social scientist and choreographer were both uncomfortable with this and made several important changes to the performance to more specifically draw attention to singlehood (for more information see Sharp and Durham DeCesaro, 2015).

MARCH 2013 PERFORMANCES IN LUBBOCK, TEXAS AND BLACKSBURG, VIRGINIA: SURVEYS

Five months after the pilot performance, the public (final) concert was performed twice (once in Lubbock, Texas and once in Blacksburg, Virginia). We collected survey (similar to the one used during the Pilot Performance) and focus group data from audiences following both performances (see Appendix B for the questions used in the focus group). The collection of survey data presented the unexpected challenge of extremely low audience response rates—the lowest that the social scientist has ever encountered in her research. Only three people completed the online survey for the Lubbock performance and only seven people completed the online survey for the Blacksburg performance. Two audience members in Lubbock and none in Blacksburg completed the paper surveys.

As noted in Chapter 3, while the social scientist was disappointed with these results, the choreographer was not as concerned, as she had no expectation that audience members would complete surveys after seeing the concert. This is not a common practice in concert dance. The choreographer discovered, though, that the information provided in the completed surveys was very valuable as a means of understanding *how* audience members were viewing the concert. For example, the March 2013 concerts' survey results indicated that participants enjoyed the performance. As one participant expressed, "I loved it. It was entertaining and provocative (and funny). I liked the dialogue that was presented before it. It is such a great idea to add." Another participant described her affective reaction: "I thought the concert was very moving. I experienced several emotions throughout. I thought the concert resonated with me." The choreographer began to prioritize audience responses and began to share the social scientist's concern about low response rates.

The focus group in Blacksburg consisted primarily of graduate students in the Human Development and Family Studies (HDFS) department. Most focus group participants, similar to the audience members who completed surveys, described the concert as "eye-opening" and "innovative." One woman in the focus group explained, "It was just so unique—I can't think of any other production that meshes the arts with the social sciences so for that purpose only I was curious." Also expressing how the performance evoked emotions for her, one participant explained, "…And so the bridesmaids with the bride - I cried a little - that captured exactly what happens—that moment of helping a friend get ready for her big deal. And it is not that you were saying anything but you could feel it—those looks that you give each other during the day are what you feel." Another participant in the focus group responded to this comment by saying, "…and when you let your hands go, that was really, it was how I felt when my best friend got married." In this case, both participants were referring to a specific moment in the dance titled "Dressed" in which two dancers release hands immediately before the bride begins to walk downstage.

A different participant added: "I feel like it was really nuanced, too, though, because they were just being supportive, they were cajoling and manipulative at the same time. Sometimes, you know, from moment to moment they might switch their motives almost. I feel like while I don't have any manipulative or controlling friends that I am aware of [laughter], …"

The HDFS graduate student focus group participants commented on how the performance highlighted the precariousness of studying relationships and marriage while also performing the bridal role. As one participant explained:

> It is a very ambivalent situation to be a social scientist who studies this [topic] but also, you know, be performing the bridal role] at the same time so I am aware. So one of my favorite scenes was when she is like "ahh…ooh…look at my precious [ring] and she gets tricked into signing this, you know, marriage contract and, you know, gets a baby thrown at her. The stork absolutely my favorite [laugher]…absolutely my favorite part. But it did a really good job of capturing the ambivalence, you know, like, we have sparkles of our very own but they come with costs and, umm, I am aware of the costs and I am aware of, you know, the meaning that is ascribed to this event but, at the same time, I am still buying into and performing it, maybe because I am not brave enough, I don't know…just it is like, just kind of what we do. It seems like the alternative of not doing it is not really an alternative so just kind of play the role but I am conscious of the role that I am playing at the same time and how preposterous things are and I'm just really trying to not be that bride because I am aware of it, I am like "no, we are not doing that"—not doing this, not doing that, no favors, you know, not buying into that crap, not impressing people, so I am trying to keep it reeled in, you know, so it can be like small scale and, you know, reasonable…

At the end of the focus group, several of the graduate students approached the social scientist to ask about the possibility of showing the dances in the undergraduate classes they taught as way to highlight course concepts. As a response to their request, we created an overview curriculum (see Chapter 7) to accompany guided viewing of the performances for college and high school students.

SEPTEMBER 2013 PERFORMANCE IN LUBBOCK, TEXAS: TEXT MESSAGING

As a corrective to the extremely low response rate to the surveys, we wrote another internal grant at our university to develop and implement a novel data collection strategy to obtain real-time audience responses through the use of audience text messaging. This data collection strategy (see Appendix C for an excerpt from the text messaging survey) was ground-breaking in many ways. First, the use of real-time responses would allow us to assess participants' *initial* responses; most social science data and dance criticism is removed (in time) from the impetus of interest. Second, we intended to collect audience responses on visceral, emotional, and cognitive levels whereas most social science inquiries gloss over visceral responses from participants. In fact, as our previous work has indicated, one important insight we gained from the focus groups was that visceral and embodied responses of audience members related to their ability to translate what they saw to their own lived experiences. We discussed this in Chapter 5 when we examined the role of resonance in affecting transformative cultural change.

The text messaging (we purchased software, called Poll Everywhere, to facilitate this) produced a high response rate: 45 people out of an audience of approximately 100 attempted to use the text messaging. Despite this improvement, other problems arose, including a systematic problem of people not completing the survey (e.g., we have 30 responses for the first question and only seven responses for the last several questions). Although the declining response rates respective to the progression through the survey could be due to a number of factors, we are fairly certain that the reason was *not* that audience members were leaving the performance after individual dances. We suspect audience fatigue from typing responses, difficulty using the software program, and/or a shift in attention from the survey to social media. To clarify the last point, some audience members might have been using text messaging for purposes other than the surveys. We had reports, for example, from some audience members that they observed other patrons using their phones to check social media sites.

Additionally, though this was not connected to the low response rate, it was evident that some audience members were trying to text while the dances were being performed rather than during the designated intervals between the dances. This was brought to our attention when dancers in the concert noted that they could see, and were distracted by, the lights from the phones' screens. Because of this complication and considering the mediocre response rate, we terminated the text messaging data collection method for future concerts. Following, though, are some of the responses to the first dance, "I Was Happy in the Pictures," that we were able to obtain from our foray into collecting data via text messaging:

"Sad"

"It had a somber tone, they seemed to be trying to get something perfect but couldn't."

"I felt like this dance was focused on the emotional side of marriage: anxiety, being overwhelmed, etc. It was abstract but nice."

"I felt very sad by this and thought they weren't happy about being married."

"Three generations of women, all trying to get free from the social stigma of what a good woman and wife should be."

This dance seemed to show the sadness and stress behind the smile we see on the wedding day."

"I felt sad but wasn't sure what the conflict was…"

Participants tended to comment more frequently on their immediate emotional reactions in the text messaging as compared to the surveys. Although several audience members wrote lengthy responses in the texts, the text messages tended to be briefer than the survey responses. While we terminated the text messaging approach to data collection, we think that scholars should continue to consider ways of obtaining real-time reactions to performances[1].

FEBRUARY 2014 PERFORMANCE IN DETROIT, MICHIGAN: SHORTER SURVEYS (AND PAYMENT) AND HYBRID FOCUS GROUP/TALKBACK SESSION

Using the shorter version of the survey we created for the text messaging as a model, we created a one-page survey (instead of the four page one we had used at the first two performances) to use at our fourth performance. We also offered $5.00 for completion of the survey. The data collection at our fourth performance yielded 27 surveys and approximately 20 people at the hybrid focus group/talkback session (guiding questions were the same as those listed in Appendix B)—our most fruitful data collection of all the previous performances. Due to the success at the fourth performance, we used the same techniques for our fifth performance. At the fifth performance, instead of $5.00 we offered (relatively rare) $2.00 bills.

With the larger response rate, we were able to identify patterns of audience members' expressed desires to know exactly how they *should* view things. For example, one participant wrote, "Really interesting. I just wish the dialogue and dances were explained better so I knew fully what was going on." Predicting that some audience members would want more explanation of the components of the concert, we had included in our pre-concert remarks, beginning with the production's premiere, some reassurance about viewers making their own

---

[1] For an interesting introduction into some possibilities associated with using technology to record sensory response, see Dr. R. Benjamin Knapp's work at the Institute for Creativity, Arts, and Technology at Virginia Tech (http://www.icat.vt.edu/users/r-benjamin-knapp).

interpretations. These remarks, which follow here, were designed to address exactly the kind of feedback noted above. It is clear, though, that some viewers still do not feel comfortable with making their own interpretations of the works.

> Tonight's performance is based on a collaborative project between a social scientist and dance choreographers. The actors' dialogues come directly from two of the social scientist's datasets. As you view the performance, you are encouraged to engage with its structure in a way that is most meaningful to you; it is your decision how to interpret the connection between the individual dialogues and dances and the organization of the concert as a whole. We encourage you to read more about the collaboration during intermission. There is more information in the lobby.

We encourage interested researchers who are considering a transdisciplinary collaboration involving dance (or other potentially abstract art form) to think about the ways in which you might preemptively, if at all, address issues of audience expectation of comprehension. Because audience engagement is a critical component of how we define the success of our own project, we continue to be concerned with audience members who indicate that they disengaged with the concert or its contents because they felt they did not understand it.

Another common idea emerging from the larger set of responses to the concert was that some men felt they could not fully relate to the performance. As one male audience member explained in his survey: "[The performance was] a very emotional interpretation of how society views marriage. A postmodern performance, with a story that all can indulge in, though, I find it hard as a male to fully relate (sadly...)." However, we would note that some younger men felt they *could* relate to the performance, especially to the dance titled "To Find My Voice." At the talkback/focus group in Detroit, one college male said about this dance: "...for me it started as way of basically seeking your own identity, trying to be different from everybody else, not be the same, just basically as a group you want to always be as a group and not like yourself, so you always want to agree with the group and not be yourself. So basically I took away from it that...anyone of us can be unique and different and we have to, of course, be brave about that."

Additionally, we are aware of a viewing trend confirming that some audience members find the overall tone of the performance negative toward marriage. Here is an example of a comment from a survey collected at the Detroit performance: "The music choices seemed sad and wishful, overall the tone seemed negative. Despite some positive quotes, the movements and "plots" were negative." Further, although only a handful of audience members commented on dances they did not like (prompted by survey questions), of these comments it is clear that the dance least liked was "I Was Happy in the Pictures," one of the most abstract dances of the entire performance.

Participants said that they were 'confused,' and they 'did not understand' the dance and that the dance was 'abrupt', 'less tangible', and they questioned whether the dance was promoting 'anti-marriage.' Our deliberate intention to *question* certain elements of marriage (and emphasized femininity) was read as a suggestion that marriage, as an institution, is "bad." This maps on to the phenomenon that the questioning normative, acceptable ways of "doing family" (Smith) or "doing femininity" results in people assuming that being critical and raising questions equates to negativity. In the single women study, for example, the social scientist found that several participants had decided to stop telling others that they didn't want to get married (or have children) because others around them had (over)interpreted their lack of desire as a direct affront to marriage and understood the single women's lack of desire for marriage (or children) as a judgment of their own choices (Sharp, "Ever Single").

APRIL 2015 PERFORMANCE IN LUBBOCK, TEXAS: SHORTER SURVEYS (AND PAYMENT) AND HYBRID FOCUS GROUP/TALKBACK SESSION

At the fifth performance, we collected 100 surveys and approximately 35 audience members stayed for the focus group/talkback session. We share some of the survey responses in Chapter 5. The responses were similar to the surveys from Detroit (shared above). The focus group/talkback session included more community members than the previous performances, and this influenced the discussion. At the talkback, one older man explained his reaction to the performance: "…the mood…was very dramatic and it seemed like it, to me as a male, from what I could gather, it seemed like there was a lot of hurt that the woman who voiced these dialogues were experiencing. As being women who had had those [societal] expectations."

In response to these comments, a woman at the same talkback spoke about the way in which the concert invoked in her an embodied experience: ":…I thought of, if you ask me one word [about the performance], I would say "touching," and as an older woman I've got some of the pain, but I also felt that even though I identified with some of the movements and all and the feelings that went along with that. And when I was younger I felt like [that]….also I came through that and I've succeeded, which is what I thought you guys demonstrated at the end. So, I really enjoyed that." At the focus group/talkback sessions, we also encourage participants to ask the social scientist, choreographer, and dancers questions. Below, we include typical questions that we get from our audience members and we offer our responses.

How does IRB work in a project like this?

The social scientist had IRB approval for the initial studies, prior to her work with the choreographer. When we began to consider the possibility of a secondary data analysis that would manifest in a theatrical performance, we wrote another IRB proposal specifically to use the original data in the performance. To ensure confidentiality, we used actors to perform the data rather than audio recordings of the original participants. We also carefully altered the text selections so no participants could be identified. Additionally, we had to write separate IRB proposals for the audience data collection. In sum, every time we have wanted to pursue something new in terms of the concert or data collection, we have written an IRB proposal for that purpose.

What was the gesture of the dancers writing near their heart[2] in the last dance, "To Find My Voice?"

We get this question every time we present the concert and at our methodological presentations, where we show the video of this dance. We typically ask the audience members for their ideas about the meaning behind the gesture in question *before* the lead choreographer responds. We have received a variety of rich interpretations over time. To give you a flavor of the ideas people offer, below we share responses from nine different audience members who attended our fifth performance and stayed for the focus group/talkback session.

> "[The gesture was]…shadowing identity. That's the name. You're writing on your name tag…"

> "…right before that dance that was used you were talking about signing away like the marriage contract…So I figured maybe it was like signing the contract but signing your name away to the husband."

> "I thought it was cross your heart and hope to die" (crowd laughs-laughter).

> "I felt like at first it was like society kind of like controlling you and marking you and saying who you are, and then by the end of the dance I felt like it was the dancer taking control…"

> "…I have a scarlet letter or you feeling…like trying to get that off…"

> "I thought they were scratching to find the inner self."

> "I thought they were the labels that we have to have. I feel like we have to have labels and they are all provided by society." (In response to this comment, another woman said, "It really became very painful to watch.")

> …"Honestly I… was it was like. I don't know…I was just like stop like a wound almost."

> " I was kinda anxious and kind of frantic emotionally."

---

[2] This gesture involves the dancers using their right hands to "write" on the left sides of their chests, as if they were writing on nametags adhered to their clothes.

Here are some responses from the lead choreographer, two dancers, and additional audience members from the Detroit focus group/talkback session:

Choreographer:
>It [writing gesture] could really be interpreted any way. When I developed the gesture I was thinking about identity and the ways in which identities [labels, positions, titles] are sometimes stuck on us like those "Hello, my name is…" tags and so the gesture is each of the dancers writing her own name or some other identity on that badge, on that "Hello my name is…" badge and then beginning to recognize what we are doing, that we are repeating and robotically identifying ourselves in some superficial way. We [the dancers] recognize this and then individually we begin to embody our actual names, our actual identities with those solos that are all different. But when [the social scientist] saw it first she thought we were writing on our hearts…

Choreographer:
>A lot of people have asked about that particular gesture and it is interesting as a dancer it didn't occur to me that it would be such a resonant gesture. So it is very interesting to get that feedback, a sort of a trending feedback…

Dancer 1:
>And just in response to that, just [be]cause I study another philosophy called Laban Movement Analysis and …he has this philosophy about how kinesthetically your body cannot lie even though your mouth is lying, so in that particular scene we are all expressing our feelings in the way that we write, the pressure in the where we stop and pause. So I found it a really rich gesture, because I think it is something that we unconsciously are doing. We know we are doing the gesture, but our timing and our effort is different for everybody so I think that is really rich.

Audience member 1:
>I noticed that everyone was different and it's just the way…the focus in the other one's mind that just kind of took me…I couldn't figure it out.

Audience member 2:
>Well, it is a contrast to writing name tags I actually, I like how you eventually write "BRAVE" here. Like, you write your core identity. I really like that part.

Dancer 2:
>I never connected that and it is really great. It is my core. [This dancer writes the word BRAVE across her stomach.]

Audience member 3:
>So at one point one dancer takes off the nametag and throws it away. Is that right?

Choreographer:
>We stop...we elect to stop writing. We recognize what we are doing and we put the pens down and we begin to dance our full names...our full identities.

Audience member 3:
>I feel like at some point someone threw down something?

Choreographer:
>It might be this [demonstrating gesture]. And that is...this is earlier in the piece and it is a gesture from, "there should be someone right there next to me and why is there not?" And at that point we all turn and look at the single woman.... So that the piece kind of moves from this expectation to recognition...."

Here are some responses from the lead choreographer to the same question asked during the Lubbock 2015 focus group/talkback session:

Choreographer:
>So ...it actually was the literal idea of filling out a paper name tag without putting much thought into it and a paper name tag with the [label] on it that's given to you that you receive passively without really questioning and you fill it out over and over and over and you never really ever think about it, because it's what you do because it's your identity and it's stuck on you right there. And then one day you decide to look at what you're writing and you do that and you stop and you're able at that point to stop writing this label that's been given to you that you don't really accept or maybe are even aware of. And instead you engage in a full body rendition of your own name. And so in the slow moments at the end we were all dancing our own names. Instead of writing a label that we didn't pick.

Audience member:
>First name or last name?

Choreographer:
>First name. (Crowd laughs) Mine's really long.

How did we create the dances?

While each dance went through a slightly different choreographic process, they all used the data in some way(s). For a more detailed description of the choreographic processes, please see Chapter 3. We include here a written response from the choreographer (identifying herself in first person) to the social scientist concerning not only the creation of the choreography for the dance titled "To Find My Voice," but also the development of other components of the dance. The social scientist had requested this information so that she could share it at a conference at which the choreographer was not present. While we haven't shared this information, at least verbatim, at our focus group/talkback sessions, we usually refer to it in general terms:

Selection of music for "To Find My Voice:"

> I worked to find music that would serve as a backdrop for rather than an integrated component of the choreography. This was deliberate and distinguishes this piece from others in the concert, such as "Dressed," in which the music and the choreography cannot exist separately from each other. I worked to find a piece of music with minimalist qualities that provided stability and consistency (no melodramatic moments). My perspective as a choreographer is that the music for "To Find My Voice" does not push the audience into receiving the dance any particular way—it allows for a significant amount of individual interpretation.

Text combined with dance in "To Find My Voice:"

> In our concert, besides in "To Find My Voice," all of the spoken word exists separately from the dances. In "To Find My Voice," I (along with [the social scientist]) wanted to communicate to the audience that the text was DIRECTLY related to the dance. That was a major reason for including the text in the actual dance itself. I also think that using text within a discrete dance might compel viewers who are less comfortable with abstract dance to engage more with what they are seeing, as the spoken word can be a source of familiarity.

How did I use the text to create actual movements in "To Find My Voice?"

> In addition to the "writing on the heart" or "name tag" moment, there are several other key moments that illustrate how my choreography emerged directly from the words. For example, the beginning of the second text excerpt reads: "Let's talk about what's wrong with these people, single people. Let's try to fix this problem that they are..." While that is being performed, four of the five dancers onstage lift our right arms up and over to our sides, as if we were putting our arms around someone next to us. We then all look in the direction at the fifth dancer, who does not have her arm out and instead is slowing collapsing to the floor. The idea here was to suggest that a woman without a partner is not a viable woman...she cannot stay afloat. (This is not my perception, obviously, but I felt it really illustrated what was being read.)

> Another section begins with the text: "And then just like the whole dating thing, pssh, God. Oh, the girl is supposed to wait for the guy to call, wait for the guy to ask you out, let the guy pay, what are you supposed to do-- just stand there and be like a doll the whole time? Are you kidding me? Like, I'm miserable...That's why I hated it: Don't put those expectations on me. And don't call me a bitch or an old maid just

because I don't follow that." That section in the dance begins with one dancer spinning through all of the others using a weight share with the wrists as points of contact. I wanted to suggest the idea of being perpetually slung around as the object of this dating game described in the text. Then, all of the dancers move to a tight clump in which four of the dancers execute small, aggressive movements toward a fifth dancer. This suggests the idea of expectations being put on women. I interpreted this physically, as an assault or attack. I think it's important to consider that these expectations are not harmless!

What was the process like for us?

This is a very common question, primarily because, we would argue, our collaboration is fairly unique in that it is transdisciplinary and integrates dance with social science. Audiences are genuinely interested in how in the world this might work. A short answer (more thoroughly detailed in Chapter 5 of this book) is that the process has been incredibly challenging. Because of those challenges, though, the process has also been incredibly rewarding. We continue to advocate for the value of paying attention to process in a transdisciplinary collaboration!

How involved were you in the choreography? (This question was specifically directed to the social scientist after the Detroit concert, so we include the verbatim response from that performance.)

Social Scientist:
    Well, the first dance I saw was: "I Was Happy in the Pictures," ...she [the choreographer] got the title of that dance from the transcript. One of the young women had said, "Well, I was happy in the pictures." ...as she [the choreographer] was making this first dance, she sent to me the videos and I asked lots of questions [and she has asked me for input]. I should also tell you that we got funding for this [from the] VP of Research there was a competition. And probably we found out we got funding in November maybe September. I don't know, but I left the country a little bit later...

Choreographer:
    Unexpectedly

Social Scientist:
    Unexpectedly. For two years.

Choreographer:
    Two years! (Crowd laughter.)

Social Scientist:
    So we did a lot of our collaboration over Skype— [NOTE: The social scientist would probably have been more involved in the creation of the dances if she had lived in the same city at the time the choreography was being created.]

Choreographer:
: Yeah.

Social Scientist:
: Through videos…And so how much was I involved? Well, I was so confused especially with the first dance! You know that's a quite abstract one for her to start with me. (Crowd laughter.) Um and remember I kept asking was that woman in three different stages. Was it three women? [The choreographer] had sent me six texts excerpts like from the data from this wedding data. And I started looking at them. I'm like oh my gosh these two are from the same person. And I had 18 different participants in that study. And then I'm like the third one's from here cause I have this almost memorized. Because I know these data so well. All six of them were from the same participant. And I'm like…what's going on?

Choreographer:
: And I'm like…they sounded good! (Crowd laughter.)

Choreographer:
: One of the things we talk about in the presentation tomorrow is that I was looking at this data for its usability. It's theatrical possibility. I wasn't looking at it based on context or who said it. I really was mining the data for my own purposes as the artistic director of the concert. And so she [the social scientist] responded that way and I thought oh-h-h-h-h. Is that an issue?

(Crowd laughter.)

Choreographer:
: And from my perspective it was not an issue. That was the artistic license that I had with this concert. And that became one of the things that we started to talk about. What are those parameters? What are those lines? Did they need to be specified before we start? How do we know to talk about that before we start?

Social Scientist:
: Yeah, so it was super troubling for me. (Crowd laughter.) So that was one of our big moments in this and goes on for a long time. Lots of questions. What should I do? And then here I am I'm like well I gotta let the audience know. So that's part of the lobby posters, so that you know some of this background…and also what do we call this? Can we even call it social science?... I had huge crises. You can hear more about them tomorrow [at the methodological talk]. (Crowd laughter.) But one thing that I definitely took a lot of comfort in was actually watching the dance and even the six excerpts that were used. There was resonance …it did map onto the angst and some struggles that several participants had shared in the study…, but when I look at data I am looking for patterns…And I am [closely] reading [the] words and I read it multiple

times. Sometimes I'll listen. But [the choreographer] was never looking for a pattern per se. And it took me a while to get over that to be honest and to even just start to understand that. That there's different ways to look at these, you know, these words [data] on paper…

CHAPTER 7

Curriculum

Image 10: "To Find My Voice," taken at March 2015 performance, Lubbock, Texas

Extending our scope beyond audience members who attended the live performance, in this chapter we discuss possibilities of integrating video-recording of the performance with course materials. Here, we provide an overview of recommendations for instructors who want to expand their teaching tools. We offer curricular content to accompany guided viewing of the *Ordinary Wars* concert via video (available at www.ordinarywars.org) or the live performance. We envision that the proposed curricular topics could be used in a variety of disciplines, including Dance, Human Development & Family Studies (HDFS), Sociology, Gender and Women's Studies, Communication Studies, Cultural Studies, and across a number of different courses within those disciplines and others. In order to avoid prescribing applicability to only a certain discipline or set of disciplines, we instead focus on content units, offering a combination of sample questions, resources to enhance discussions, and written activities to be used within the classroom and beyond as we continue to encourage possibilities of this project to advance transformative cultural change.[1]

---

[1] For example, the social scientist has discussed the wedding study and the dances accompanying the wedding study at a public library in the UK. Her presentation was part of a larger series of community engagement.

CONTENT UNITS AND SAMPLE QUESTIONS:

Ordinary Wars is especially applicable to curricular content concerning weddings, marriage, motherhood, singlehood, performativity, sex/gender development, choreography, and research methods. We encourage instructors to think about using the dances separately or using the entire concert. The social scientist and one of the secondary choreographers used the entire concert in their courses, but the social scientist and the primary choreographer typically only show one dance when they present at conferences. Limiting the focus to one dance can be a highly effective way to showcase particular topics/content.

Content Unit: Weddings

The *Ordinary Wars* concert helps showcase how weddings, wifehood, singlehood, femininity, and sexuality are performances. Two of the dances, "I Was Happy in the Pictures" and "Dressed" highlight the ways in which the wedding itself is a performance. Some scholars push further here, arguing that contemporary weddings may be considered a "spectacle" (Ingraham). The roles of bride, bridesmaids, and mother of the bride are all socially scripted and women in these roles are expected to perform "bridal femininity," which includes "emphasized femininity"—femininity that is hyperfeminine and adhering to traditional notions of women (Cornell). In contrast, single women are thought to perform "pariah femininity"—classified as a threat to the larger social order (see Finkey).

As one participant explained in a focus group after seeing *Ordinary Wars*: "Watching a performance about weddings made me realize that in a way, weddings themselves are performances, and so I kind of took a more negative spin to what you [another participant in the focus group] were describing. You were crying and I was like 'omigosh, so fake—you are just doing it because that is just what everyone does.'" In this comment, the participant is re-thinking scripted roles embedded in conventional weddings, and she begins to question authenticity of people fulfilling such roles. She is starting to raise larger questions about societal expectations for affective responses.

Sample Questions for Examining the Topic of Weddings:
- What is involved in wedding performance? How is this conveyed in the concert?
- Who is performing and what is being performed?
- What are examples of "emphasized femininity" in the dance performance? Did you notice these in the choreography? The design? The dialogues?
- What are some examples of "pariah femininity" in the dance performance? Did you notice these in the choreography? The design? The dialogues?
- How is the symbolism of a wedding dress, an engagement ring, and the contract with the state relevant to the performance embedded in weddings?

- Consider the idea of the "wedding as a spectacle." What does this mean? Is this an accurate description of weddings right now? Explain.
- How is perfectionism operating in the performance of bridal femininity[2]?

Content Unit: Marriage and Motherhood

The dances titled "Dressed" and "The Cowboy, the Lawyer, and the Stork" focus on and question marriage as an institution (see Chapter 4 for a brief discussion of how this questioning is read by audiences as claiming that marriage is negative). The second part of "Dressed" showcases women judging the new wife as she attempts to "be sexy," cook and clean, and care for an infant. This dance highlights residual yet still prevalent ideas about what a wife "should be" and visually clarifies the intense pressure many wives face as they enact their new role. "The Cowboy, The Lawyer, and The Stork" helps showcase societal pressure, materialism (focus on an engagement ring), how marriage is a contract with the state, and the overbearing weight of negotiating responsibilities linked with wifehood (and ensuing motherhood).

We recommend pairing ideas from any of the aforementioned dances with Stephanie Coontz' book *Marriage, A History* or any number of scholarly articles about marriage, including the social scientist's article, "Betty Crocker versus Betty Friedan: Becoming a Wife in West Texas" (Sharp), based on the wedding /marriage study used in *Ordinary Wars*. The abstract is below:

> In this paper, deploying Betty Friedan's (1963) Feminine Mystique and the fictional American icon Betty Crocker within a post-structural feminist analysis, the author analyzes a social science dataset investigating how 18 contemporary wives think about wifehood. Crocker and Friedan are emblematic of the cultural DNA that make up wifehood: the mythical Betty Crocker represents the happy, traditional housewife of the 1950's and Betty Friedan offers a critique of the happy, traditional housewife figure. Thinking about historical trends, in the 1950's-60's, femininity and families were rigidly prescribed and, thus, largely unquestioned. In the 21st century, with the influx of postmodernism, post-feminism, and neo-liberal discourses, prescriptions for femininity and families are thought to be less rigid—but are they? The contemporary wives' identity negotiations mapped on to both Betty Crocker and Betty Friedan, but remained anchored in the Betty Crocker image.

---

[2] We also recommend pairing the dance titled "Dressed" with the social scientist's and her colleague's article titled, "*Make sure you get at least a piece of your own cake*": Stress, Perfectionism, and the Princess/Bridezilla Binary. In this paper, they reveal what they call "an untenable binary: princess and bridezilla" as well as the "effortless perfection" of everyday femininity, felt more acutely when performing "bridal femininity." The princess image depicts a passive, subdued, and responding (e.g., waiting for her prince to notice and chose her) bride. Bridezilla, on the hand, embodies the ability to *resist* 'emphasized femininity' – through publically showing anger, strain, and stress.

The dance titled "With Doubt" and, to some extent, excerpts from "Dressed" (described above) directly question a social expectation that all women will or want to become mothers. "With Doubt" is one of the more abstract works in the concert. Viewers generally identify with a particular movement repeated frequently through the dance that suggests holding and rocking a baby. A much more direct reference to motherhood comes in the second half of "Dressed," as one of the props used is a baby doll (deliberately unrealistic-looking).

Sample Questions for Examining Marriage and Motherhood:

- How are the concepts of the "Motherhood Mandate" and "compulsory heterosexuality" relevant to the concert? To any particular dance or dialogue?
- How is marriage as a highly valued relationship linked to the performance?
- How is motherhood suggested or questioned in the performance? What kind of "symbols" in the dances did you read as connected to motherhood? Were any of these movement symbols? If so, explain why you understood them as connected to motherhood.
- How is the compulsion to cook/nurture reflected (or not reflected) in any of the dances?
- How does the cooking/cleaning map on to wider gendered patterns in contemporary families?
- How important is a name change? What parts of the concert, if any, did you think addressed this?
- How is internalized sexism revealed in the performance?
- How is being a wife considered a performance?

Content Unit: Singlehood

The dances titled "A Thin Line," "With Doubt," and "To Find My Voice" feature single women's experiences. Issues of timing, age, stigma, choice, authenticity, conformity/non-conformity, and desire are underscored in the dances. We recommend pairing the dances with the literature on single women, including Bella DePaulo's work, and the social scientist's work, which keeps the focus on timing (i.e., personal and societal timetables) and ever-single women's thinking about marriage and children. The social scientist purposely selects samples of women living during their "prime family-building" years (25 to 40's), which, theoretically, are accompanied by heightened contemplation of marriage/children. She argues that this time period can be considered a "liminoid" period in ever-single women's development (Sharp and Ganong, "I'm a Loser").

One premise in the social scientist's work is that the language and concepts in the life course perspective do not adequately capture ever-single women's lives as they negotiate their self-identities within the context of the SNAF (Standard North American Family; Smith). Focusing on both ontological and social timing, in her first research project on ever-single women, the social scientist used the word "missed" to capture the experience of not marrying by the age most of their peers married (Sharp and Ganong). She argued that "missed" was a more accurate description than "off-time" transitions (life course language) because "off-time" signified that a person had actually experienced the transition, albeit later (or earlier) than most of her peers. In the case of the women in her initial study, they had not been married, so they could not be classified as "off-time" in the ways that "off-time" is typically used in life course framing. Women who "missed" the marital transition (i.e., women who had wanted to marry within the normative social timetables) experienced ambiguity (without the normative timetable to structure/predict their lives, they wished they knew how their lives would turn out) and ambivalence (wavering back and forth about being satisfied with their choices and their current lives). The social scientist considered the theoretical framing of ambiguous loss—the parameters of whether the women would (at some point) marry were unclear, creating an experience without closure (Boss).

In "A Thin Line," viewers might be directed to this lack of "closure" by considering the symbol of the tightrope and how that might be a metaphor for different aspects of lived singlehood. Viewers might also deliberately focus on the amount of time that the two dancers move completely separately from each other, without acknowledgement, and what that might suggest concerning singlehood and "belonging."

Again, as one of the most abstract works in the concert, "With Doubt" carries with it significant potential for varied meaning making. Here, instructors might consider a freewriting exercise designed to encourage students to thoroughly explore personal responses to this particular dance, as there are few identifiable "images" to follow. The same would be true for the dance titled "To Find My Voice," except that this dance includes, in its sound score, recorded text from the original participants' data (more thoroughly described in Chapter 3).

Sample Questions for Examining Singlehood:

- How is singlehood a performance?
- How is the "writing your name gesture" linked to women's experiences and conventional notions of femininity?
- Why was "brave" written on the women's bodies? Was this trying to argue that married women are not brave?
- Is not wanting marriage and/or children an affront to SNAF?
- How is the dialogue "I'm like, "Crap! I better hurry up and have a child really quick, like in the next couple of years, because, like, I'm already halfway through 32-and so I'm 33 and da-da-da-da-da, and how old will I be when this kid graduates from high school?" and, …. "Shit, I better have one right now!" related to life course perspective?
- How are binaries presented?
- How is the invisibility of singleness (e.g. props, advertising, etc.) reflected (or not reflected) in the concert?

Content Unit: Performativity

Ordinary Wars presents performativity both overtly and discreetly. Using Butler's original explanation of performativity, two of the dances in the concert draw on the ways in which femininity, marriage, and heterosexuality are socially (mundanely) performed (acted), thereby constituting their cultural meanings. Those dances are "Dressed" and "The Cowboy, the Lawyer, and the Stork." In "Dressed" (Part 1), elements of the cultural performativity of a wedding day (or getting married or bride or becoming a bride) are presented to the audience. This happens through the choreographed overemphasis on things like "the dress," "the rabid bridesmaids," and "the transformation."

In "Dressed" (Part 2), performativity is presented again, though with an emphasis on how the identity of "wife" is culturally constructed. Again, through the use of choreographed overemphasis on certain acts and actions associated with being a "good wife," we present the identity of a married woman as a static concept derived from the ability to correctly execute socially constructed expectations. Finally, in "The Cowboy, the Lawyer, and the Stork," the concept of marriage is problematized through the presentation of different elements of gender performativity traditionally associated with heterosexual marriage. In this dance, satire and sarcasm are used most directly so that the elements of performativity are not just overemphasized but are totally ridiculed.

Arguably, what makes these dances work is that viewers are aware of the ways in which gender performativity (within the specific context of marriage) functions culturally and are able to identify that performativity when it is presented on stage. This means that our audiences somehow recognize gender, femininity, and marriage as performed acts and are able to understand that the dances are designed to question the legitimacy of those acts through the use of theatrical humor. In this way, *Ordinary Wars* overtly uses Butler's theory of performativity within a theatrical construct.

Some more discreet questions about performativity in performance emerge when considering the concert from a meta-theatrical perspective. It is necessary to question whether the effectiveness of using performativity in *Ordinary Wars* to critique culturally defined expectations of gender and marriage is compromised: generally, when an audience attends a performance, that audience expects to suspend its reality for the duration of the performance event. Does this mean that our critique is somehow less valid because the audience encounters it in a space traditionally "separated" from reality? Perhaps the most critical question is whether presenting our critiques and questions in the context of a formal concert somehow absolves the audience members of applying those critiques and questions to their everyday experiences. If an audience member simply wants to be entertained by the performance, it is possible no questioning/reflections occur and/or that reiterations of cultural norms are effectively reproduced. Asked more directly: is it possible that the concert reifies the very cultural stereotypes that we have tried to question by presenting those concepts within a construct that is traditionally associated with entertainment?

Content Unit: Sex/Gender Development

For a content unit on sex/gender development, we move away from referencing specific dances and instead tie the overall concert to a set of recommended readings. The questions below are intended to accompany reflection on the concert as a whole and synthesis of ideas and themes emerging from the concert and class readings.

Sample questions for examining the topics of sex/gender development:

1. Overall, what are your impressions of the concert? What emotional and/or physical reactions did it have for you? [There are no right or wrong answers, so it is fine if you feel apathetic or sad or elated or several contradictory emotions.]
2. What messages about sex/gender did you take away from the concert? What questions did the concert raise for you?
3. In broad terms, how is the concert relevant to our course work?
4. Grounding your response in the first set of readings and discussions*, how are the basic concepts, assumptions, and myths relevant to the concert?
5. Grounding your response in the second set of readings and discussions**, provide an example of sex/gender stereotypes operating in the concert. Did the concert help disrupt this assumption/myth or perpetuate it? Explain.
6. How might you connect the idea that sex/gender is a performance to *Ordinary Wars*? Explain.
7. What theoretical perspective (s) from the readings and discussions might best apply to the concert? Justify your answer by specifically tying the theory to the concert (or portions of the concert).
8. How are emphasized femininity and hegemonic heterosexuality at work?
9. In the concert, in what ways were binaries disrupted and/or reproduced? Give an example.
10. Select one of the authors from our readings or textbook. What would the author say about this performance? What aspects do you think s/he would like and what concerns/cautions do you think s/he would make? What informs your conclusions?
11. Any other comments or reactions you would like to share?

*Readings Included:

Fausto-Sterling, Anne. "The Five Sexes, Revisited." *The Sciences* 40.4 (2000): 18–23.

Fine, Cordelia. Delusions of gender: How our minds, society, and neurosexism create difference. WW Norton & Company, 2010.

Ortner, Sherry B., Michelle Zimbalist Rosaldo, and Louise Lamphere. "Woman, Culture, and Society." *Woman, Culture and Society* (1974).

Walter, Natasha. *Living dolls: The Return of Sexism*. Hachette, UK, 2011.

****Readings Included:*

Fine, Cordelia. Delusions of gender: How our minds, society, and neurosexism create difference. WW Norton & Company, 2010.

Martin, Emily. "The egg and the sperm: How science has constructed a romance based on stereotypical male-female roles." Signs 16.3 (1991): 485-501.

Walter, Natasha. Living dolls: The return of sexism. Hachette, UK, 2011.

Weisstein, Naomi. "Psychology constructs the female." Journal of Social Education 35 (1971): 362-373.

Content Unit: Choreography

Using words as the basis or stimulus for choreography is not a new approach to making dance. Frequently, students in choreography courses investigate the use of language in dance-making, working with spoken word and/or written text in a variety of ways. For emerging choreographers, *Ordinary Wars* offers an opportunity to observe and question the ways in which text manifests in movement. Choreography students can use the dances not only to analyze the various relationships between text and movement present in *Ordinary Wars,* but they can also begin to assess their own patterns of recognition, a valuable piece of information for any choreographer. Some questions for students are:

Sample Questions for Use in a Choreography Course:

- What gestures in the choreography do you identify as "literal?" Why? What does that tell you about larger cultural patterns?
- Review the text excerpts used as stimuli for the dance "I Was Happy in the Pictures." Do you "recognize" those excerpts in the choreography? How?
- Consider the spoken word in the dance "To Find My Voice." Create your own movement motif using one of the text excerpts. Describe your choreographic process.

Content Unit: Research Methods

The project offers a host of methodological issues for students to discuss and analyze and has worked as an effective teaching tool in the social scientist's graduate-level qualitative methods course. Although the social scientist's students were able to view the live performance during the semester she taught the course, the video of the performance can also be used. Below, we offer a list of methodological concepts and questions that link to the *Ordinary Wars* project and are designed for use in a Research Methods course.

Sample Questions for Use in a Research Methods Course:
- What is data? Who gets to decide?
- What constitutes a secondary data analysis of qualitative research?
- How do disciplinary classifications and associated expectations affect research processes?
- What is a kinesthetic analysis?
- What data are rejected/discarded in research? Is this important to examine?
- What constitutes a transdisciplinary project?
- How can discomfort be used as a methodological approach?
- How is re-presenting distinct from representing?
- What is reality/realities and whose realities get privileged in this project?
- What is the importance of pilot data in transdisciplinary work?
- What is good research? How do we evaluate transdisciplinary work?
- What is disciplinary humility?

Content Unit: Qualitative Methods

In the social scientist's graduate qualitative methods course, she required that her students attend either the dress rehearsal or the performance of *Ordinary Wars* and write a paper reflecting on the performance. She provided students with guiding questions (see below). Prior to attending the performance, students were also asked to read one of the articles from the project: Durham DeCesaro, G., and E. A. Sharp. "Immersion in the muddy waters: a collaboration between a social scientist and a dance choreographer." *The International Journal of Social, Political and Community Agendas in the Arts* 7 (2014): 57-66.

Sample questions for a qualitative methods course:
- Overall, what are your impressions of the performance? What were your reactions?
- What messages did you take away from the performance? What methodological questions did the performance raise for you?
- How did you choose to interpret the structure the performance?
- In broad terms, how is the performance related to our coursework?
- What do you think Daly* would say about the performance? Explain.
- Grounding your response in the readings and discussion about epistemology, how would you classify the performance? Explain how you came to this conclusion.
- What ontological (if any) questions did this raise for you?
- Summarize what you learned from your audience observations. Describe how your observation work relates to strategies/advice from authors in our course.
- Any other comments or reactions you would like to share?

* Daly, Kerry J. Qualitative methods for family studies and human development. Sage Publications, (2007).

EVIDENCE OF CURRICULAR EFFECTIVENESS

As aforementioned, in two of her HDFS graduate courses cross-listed with Women's Studies (Sex/Gender Development and Qualitative Methods), the social scientist has already experimented with pairing *Ordinary Wars* with course material. The use of *Ordinary Wars* in her classes has been highly effective. Being able to draw on *Ordinary Wars* in both a content course (i.e. Sex/Gender Development) and a methodological course (i.e., Qualitative Research Methods) is indicative of the versatility of the project. We offer a sample of students' engagement with *Ordinary Wars* using written responses from their coursework below:

Binaries (Drawing on Poststructural Thought):

"…binaries were disrupted by showing that these feminine characteristics are not natural and we are taught to perform them. While I may know all of this from the amount of reading I do within feminism (inside and outside of this class) seeing socialization being performed helped break down binaries more so than any reading I have ever done. Perhaps readings gave me a framework for which to view the performances, but they were incredibly powerful. The ability to watch this socialization process through such simplistic movements and acting really highlighted the absurdity of binaries for me."

Highlighting the Affective Turn in Social Science:

"I think it [the performance] is an excellent creation that allows portraying women's lives and realities through art. I believe art, as a symbolic representation of ideas, allows the audience to connect in different ways with those stories and create personal interpretations. Also, it permits reflection without predisposing certain reactions/responses. Regarding my emotional reactions, I felt very engaged with the performance. Every dance elicited different reactions in me: From anger to feeling happy, from rejection to feeling identified with some stories, from feeling apathetic to empathetic. This "roller coaster" of emotions made me felt engaged all the time."

Judgment of Women/Internalized Sexism:

"The overall message I came away with is that women are constantly judged - judged by their relationship status, judged by their desire to have children, and judged by men and women, both. The last message I took from the performance was that women need to carry on with who they are and to do what they need to be brave and stand their ground when society tries to persuade them otherwise. The significance regarding the performer writing brave on her body was very timely especially in this current environment when so many messages, coming from a variety of avenues, about how women should be are still traditionally based."

Reflection and Relevance

"...Not a day has gone by since I saw this performance that I haven't thought about it. As a feminist in many activities that are male dominated (debate, academics and even my family life) *Ordinary Wars* spoke volumes to me...Furthermore, it reminded me why I am doing what I do. It is inspiring to see you take your research out of textbooks and journals and into the real world."

Discovering that the *Ordinary Wars* concert has such a powerful impact on our audience members is gratifying. Further, it is not an overstatement to characterize the impact of the project on us, as transdisciplinary researchers and within our home disciplines, as profound. In our final chapter, to extend the reflections we have already offered in previous chapters, we share focused reflections on how the project has affected us and we identify our future goals.

CHAPTER 8

Roads Ahead: Choosing Pathways of Discomfort and Humility

Image 11: The social scientist (left) and the choreographer (right) at Talkback/Focus Group, April 15, 2015 Lubbock, Texas. Performance commissioned by Texas Tech University's Women's Studies Program

Our transdisciplinary project thus far has been an exhilarating journey—a journey rife with road blocks, stops, and slow zones, as well as high speeds and vast, open roads—evoking a sense of endless possibilities. Of course, the journey is not over and we don't see an end in sight. A truism of transdisciplinary work is that it does not afford a neatly defined, distinct ending. In other forms of collaborative research when the focus is primarily on the research product, once the product is "produced," the project is generally considered complete, though other scholars certainly may continue to re-visit and comment on their projects. In transdisciplinary work, though, the "product" is not as tightly contained. We have been surprised by the expansiveness of our work together. Over three and a half years ago, in our initial grant proposal, we had our sights set on a project with clear(er) boundaries. We could not have fully imagined the extent to which we would be engaged across such wide spaces within our disciplines, across disciplines, in the academy, and beyond.

As we continue to work together to refine and revise *Ordinary Wars*, we also continue to reflexively examine our working process. Doing that allows us to identify practices that might be helpful if replicated or used as models for other collaborations. As we've noted in this book, our aim is not to prescribe a set of uniform methodological and/or practical procedures, but rather to raise incisive questions and to provide a framework of support to help researchers navigate challenges unique to transdisciplinary work.

Our Specific Next Steps Include:

- Analyzing the "rejected" data from the initial transcripts. We are examining both the choreographer's and the social scientist's rejection (e.g., Sharp and Durham DeCesaro, "What Does Rejection") of data and of other components of the project. For example, the social scientist is reconsidering her rejection of the "kidnapping" expert from Chapter 1 of this book.
- Sending the video link to the social scientist's initial participants and soliciting their responses—we mentioned this idea in Chapter 5.
- Based on a sociologist's suggestion in one of our methodological talks, inviting a qualitative scholar on our campus to interview us jointly about the project.
- Working with choreographers and dance faculty to develop a full curriculum for dancers and choreographers to accompany the video.
- Evaluating the curriculum described in Chapter 7.
- Inspired by the JUSTICE PROJECT (see Sharp, Johnson, and Wesley), developing an intervention aimed at inviting young women to embody ideas from the performance by engaging in a dance workshop.

We leave the reader with what we consider to be key contributions to the growing field of transdisciplinary research. First, we refer back to our identification and encouragement of two frameworks: *methodology of discomfort* and *disciplinary humility*. Both of these frameworks operate on central principles of understanding, questioning, reinforcing, critiquing, and reframing the ways in which we, as academics, understand ourselves and our fields of study within the larger academy. Additionally, we promote the idea of pushing the *trans* portion of the term transdisciplinary. We advocate this type of work as a means of fostering *trans*formative change: academic, disciplinary, personal, and cultural.

Finally, we return to that early need to "correctly" categorize our work. We suggest, for the reader and for prospective transdisciplinary researchers, that not fitting neatly into an existing, defined academic and/or artistic category is a sign that you're on the right track. It is frustrating, to be sure, not to have an easily understood response when asked: "What kind of research is this?" However, part of what makes transdisciplinary research so valuable is its fundamental questioning of existing boundaries and paradigms. To that end, we continue to find overlaps between our ways of working and those described as arts-based research and performative social science and, of course, dance and social science. We choose, though, to focus less on the disciplinary aspects that constitute our collaboration and more on the unique opportunities and challenges inherent in embracing our transdisciplinary identity.

We continue to be surprised, challenged, and impressed by what this journey has offered us thus far and where it continues to take us. We are enthusiastic about supporting the paths of others interested in finding in our project a set of tools for their own work, their classrooms, or their transdisciplinary projects. Readers who are interested in learning more about *Ordinary Wars,* the researchers, or transdisciplinary collaborations involving dance and/or social science might consider contacting us at: www.ordinarywars.org.

Our often dramatic and sometimes mundane battles in our own ordinary wars of working on this transdisciplinary project have been exhausting, but our rewards have been incomparable. It is our hope that, in publicizing our discomfort, negotiations, defeats, and victories, our project encourages more transdisciplinary collaborations between social scientists and dance choreographers (and other artists), and more investment in the kind of critical, disciplinary questioning that has emerged in our own process. Has this been a safe gamble? No, not at all. With high risks, though, there is potential for high rewards... and we think we have experienced extraordinary victories.

WORKS CITED

Alexander, B.K. "Performance Ethnography: The Reenacting and Inciting of Culture." *Strategies of Qualitative Inquiry*. Eds. Norman K. Denzin and Yvonna S. Lincoln. Thousand Oaks, CA: Sage, 2007. 75-118. Print.

Arditti, Joyce A., Jennifer Lambert-Shute, and Karen Joest. "Saturday Morning at the Jail: Implications of Incarceration for Families and Children." *Family Relations* 52.3 (2003): 195-204. Print.

Austin, Ann E., and Roger G. Baldwin. "Faculty Collaboration: Enhancing the Quality of Scholarship and Teaching." *ASHE-ERIC Higher Education Report* 7. (1991): n.pag. Web. May 2014.

Bagley, Carl. "Educational Ethnography as Performance Art: Towards a Sensuous Feeling and Knowing." *Qualitative Research* 8.1 (2008): 53-72. Print.

Bagley, Carl, and MaryBeth Cancienne, eds. *Dancing the Data*. New York, NY: Peter Lang Publishing, Inc, 2002. Print.

Baldwin, Roger G. and Deborah A. Chang. "Collaborating to Learn, Learning to Collaborate." *Peer Review* 9.4 (2007): 26. Print.

Barone, Tom, and Elliot W. Eisner. *Arts Based Research*. London: Sage, 2012. Print.

Bean, Robert. "Artifacts of Research." *Canadian Review of Art Education: Research and Issues* 34 (2007): 69-87. Print.

Benhabib, Seyla, and Drucilla Cornell. *Feminism as Critique: On the Politics of Gender*. Minneapolis: University of Minnesota Press, 1987. Print.

Boss, Pauline. *Ambiguous Loss: Learning to Live With Unresolved Grief*. Cambridge, MA: Harvard University Press, 2009. Print.

Blumenfeld-Jones, Donald. "If I Could Have Said It, I Would Have." *Dancing the Data*. Eds. Carl Bagley and MaryBeth Cancienne. New York: Peter Lang Publishing, 2002. 90-104. Print.

Blumenfeld-Jones, Donald. "Dance, Choreography, and Social Science Research." *The Handbook of the Arts in Qualitative Research*. Eds. J.G. Knowles and A. L. Cole. Thousand Oaks, CA: Sage, 2008. 175-184. Print.

Braidotti, Rosi. *The Posthuman*. Cambridge, UK: Polity Press, 2013. Print.

Butler, Judith. "Performative Acts and Gender Constitution: An Essay in Phenomenology and Feminist Theory." *Theatre Journal* 40.4 (1988): 519-531. Print.

Charmaz, Kathy. "Grounded Theory: Objectivist and Constructivist Methods." *Handbook of Qualitative Research*. Eds. Norman K. Denzin and Yvonna S. Lincoln. Thousand Oaks, CA: Sage. 2008. 509-535. Print.

Cole, A. L., and J. G. Knowles. "Arts-Informed Research." *The Handbook of the Arts in Qualitative Research*. Eds. J.G. Knowles and A. L. Cole. Thousand Oaks, CA: Sage, 2008. 56-70. Print.

Coontz, Stephanie. *Marriage, a History: How Love Conquered Marriage*. New York: Penguin, 2006. Print.

Cornell, R. W. *Gender and Power: Society, the Person and Sexual Politics*. Redwood City, CA: Stanford University Press, 1997. Print.

Denzin, Norman K., and Yvonna S. Lincoln. "Introduction: Entering the Field of Qualitative Research." *Strategies of Qualitative Inquiry*. Eds. Norman K. Denzin and Yvonna S. Lincoln. Thousand Oaks, CA: Sage, 1998. 1-34. Print.

DeSantis, Lydia, and Doris Noel Ugarriza. "The Concept of Theme as Used in Qualitative Nursing Research." *Western Journal of Nursing Research* 22.3 (2000): 351-372. Print.

Durham DeCesaro, Genevieve, and Elizabeth A. Sharp. "Almost Drowning: Data as a Troubling Anchor in a Dance/Social Science Collaboration." *International Journal of Qualitative Methods* 13 (2014): 411-421. Web. July 2014.

Durham DeCesaro, Genevieve, and Elizabeth A. Sharp. "Immersion in the Muddy Waters: A Collaboration Between a Social Scientist and a Dance Choreographer." *The International Journal of Social, Political and Community Agendas in the Arts* 7.3 (2014): 57-66. Web. January 2015.

DePaulo, Bella M., and Wendy L. Morris. "Singles in Society and in Science." *Psychological Inquiry* 16.2-3 (2005): 57-83. Print.

Finley, S. "Arts-based Research." *The Handbook of the Arts in Qualitative Research*. Eds. J.G. Knowles and A. L. Cole. Thousand Oaks, CA: Sage, 2008. 71-82. Print.

Works Cited

Finkey, Nancy, J. "Skating Femininity: Gender Maneuvering in Women's Roller Derby." *Journal of Contemporary Ethnography* 39 (2010): 359-387. Print.

Friedan, Betty. *The Feminine Mystique.* New York: WW Norton & Company, 1963. Print.

Gergen, Kenneth J., and Mary M. Gergen. "Mischief, Mystery, and Moments That Matter Vistas of Performative Inquiry." *Qualitative Inquiry* 20.2 (2014): 213-221. Print.

Gergen, Mary and Kenneth J. Gergen. *Playing with Purpose: Adventures in Performative Social Science.* Walnut Creek, CA: Left Press, 2012. Print.

Gergen, Mary and Kenneth J. Gergen. "Performative Social Science and Psychology." *Forum: Qualitative Social Research/Qualitative Sozialforschung* 12.1 (2010): n.pag. January 2015.

Gergen, Mary, and Kip Jones. "Editorial: A Conversation about Performative Social Science." *Forum: Qualitative Social Research/Qualitative Sozialforschung* 9 (2008): 43-57. Web. January 2015.

Gilgun, Jane F. "Enduring Themes of Qualitative Family Research." *Journal of Family Theory & Review* 4.2 (2012): 80-95. Web. December 2015.

Goldstein, Tara, Julia Gray, Jennifer Salisbury, and Pamela Snell. "When Qualitative Research Meets Theater The Complexities of Performed Ethnography and Research-Informed Theater Project Design." *Qualitative Inquiry* 20.5 (2014): 674-685. Print.

Goffman, Erving. *The Presentation of Self in Everyday Life.* New York: Anchor Books, 1959. Print.

Greene, Maxine. *Landscapes of Learning.* New York: Teachers College Press, 1978. Print.

Guiney Yallop, John, Irene Lopez de Vallejo and Peter Wright. "Editorial: Overview of the Performance Social Science Special Issue." *Forum: Qualitative Social Research/Qualitative Sozialforschung* 9.2 (2008): n.pag. January 2015.

Hodgins, Michael J., and Katherine M. Boydell. "Interrogating Ourselves: Reflections on Arts-Based Health Research." *Forum: Qualitative Social Research/Qualitative Sozialforschung* 15.1 (2013): n.pag. January 2015.

Humphrey, Doris. *The Art of Making Dances.* Hightstown, NJ: Princeton Book Company, 1959. Print.

Ingraham, Chris. *White Weddings: Romancing Heterosexuality in Popular Culture*. New York: Routledge, 2008. Print.

Jackson, Stevi. "Gender, Sexuality and Heterosexuality: The Complexity (and Limits) of Heteronormativity." *Feminist Theory* 7.1 (2006): 105-121. Print.

Jackson, Tony. "The Dialogic and the Aesthetic: Some Reflections on Theatre as a Learning Medium." *The Journal of Aesthetic Education* 39.4 (2005): 104-118. Print.

Jeffrey, Paul. "Smoothing the Waters: Observations on the Process of Cross-Disciplinary Research Collaboration." *Social Studies of Science* 33.4 (2003): 539-562. Print.

Jones, Kip, and Patricia Leavy. "A Conversation Between Kip Jones and Patricia Leavy: Arts-Based Research, Performative Social Science and Working on the Margins." *The Qualitative Report*, 19.19 (2014): 1-7. Web. August 2014.

Kezar, A. "Redesigning for Collaboration with Higher Education Institutions: An Exploration into the Developmental Process." *Research in Higher Education,* 46 (2005): 809-860. Print.

Knowles, J.G. and A. L. Cole, eds. *The Handbook of the Arts in Qualitative Research.* Thousand Oaks, CA: Sage, 2008. Print.

Koelsch, Stefan. *Brain and Music*. New York: John Wiley & Sons, 2012. Print.

Koelsch, Stefan, and Thomas Stegemann. "The Brain and Positive Biological Effects in Healthy and Clinical Populations." *Music, Health, and Wellbeing* (2012): 436-456. Print.

LaFreniere, Darquise, et al., "Performing the Human Subject: Arts-Based Knowledge Dissemination in Health Research." *Journal of Applied Arts & Health,* 3 (2013): 243-257. Print.

Lather, Patti. "Issues of Validity in Openly Ideological Research: Between a Rock and a Soft Place." *Interchange* 17.4 (1986): 63-84. Print.

Lavender, Larry. *Dancers Talking Dance: Critical Evaluation in the Choreography Class*. Champaign, IL: Human Kinetics, 1996. Print.

Leavy, Patricia. *Method Meets Art: Arts-Based Research*. New York: The Guilford Press, 2009. Print.

Lloyd, Sally A., Rebecca L. Warner, Kristine M. Baber and Donna Sollie. "Activism in the Academy: Constructing/Negotiating Feminist Leadership." *Handbook of Feminist Family Studies*. Eds. Sally A. Lloyd,

April. L. Few, and Katherine Allen. Thousand Oaks, CA: Sage, 2009. 292-303. Print.

Lloyd, Sally A., Beth C. Emery, and Suzanne Klatt. "Discovering Women's Agency in Response to Intimate Partner Violence." *Handbook of Feminist Family Studies*. Eds. Sally A. Lloyd, April. L. Few, and Katherine Allen. Thousand Oaks, CA: Sage, 2009. 264-278. Print.

McNiff, Shaun. "Art-Based Research." *The Handbook of the Arts in Qualitative Research*. Eds. J.G. Knowles and A. L. Cole. Thousand Oaks, CA: Sage, 2008. 29-40. Print.

Morse, Janice M., Michael Barrett, Maria Mayan, Karin Olson, and Jude Spiers. "Verification Strategies for Establishing Reliability and Validity in Qualitative Research." *International Journal of Qualitative Methods* 1.2 (2008): 13-22. Web. July 2014.

Pariser, David. "Arts-Based Research: Trojan Horses and Shibboleths. The Liabilities of a Hybrid Research Approach. What Hath Eisner Wrought?" *Canadian Review of Art Education: Research and Issues* 36 (2009): 1-18. Print.

Piercy, Fred P. and Kristen Benson. "Aesthetic Forms of Data Representation in Qualitative Family Therapy Research." *Journal of Marital and Family Therapy* 31 (2005). 107-119. Print.

Pink, Sarah. *Doing Sensory Ethnography*. London, UK: Sage, 2009. Print.

Risman, Barbara J. "Gender as a Social Structure Theory Wrestling with Activism." *Gender & Society* 18.4 (2004): 429-450. Print.

Rumbold, Jean, Patricia Fenner, and Janine Brophy-Dixon. "The Risks of Representation: Dilemmas and Opportunities in Art-Based Research." *Journal of Applied Arts & Health* 3.1 (2012): 67-78. Print.

Sharp, Elizabeth. A. "Ever Single Women in Their 20's and 30's Who Resist Conventional Family Ideologies." National Council on Family Relations Annual Conference. Phoenix, AZ. November 2012. Conference Presentation.

Sharp, Elizabeth A. "Betty Crocker vs. Betty Friedan: Becoming a Wife in West Texas." Women as Wives & Workers: Marking Fifty Years of *The Feminine Mystique* Conference. University of London, London, UK. November 2013. Conference Presentation.

Sharp, Elizabeth A. and Genevieve Durham DeCesaro. "Modeling Innovative Methodological Practices in a Dance/Family Studies Transdisciplinary Project." *Journal of Family Theory & Review* 7.4 (2015) 367–380. Print.

Sharp, Elizabeth A. and Genevieve Durham DeCesaro. "What Does Rejection Have to Do With it? Toward an Innovative, Kinesthetic Analysis of Qualitative Data." *Forum: Qualitative Social Research/Qualitative Sozialforschung* 14.2 (2013): n.pag August 2014.

Sharp, Elizabeth A. and Larry Ganong. " 'I'm a Loser, I'm Not Married, Let's Just All Look at Me:' Ever Single Women's Perceptions of their Social Environment." *Journal of Family Issues* 32 (2011): 956–980. Print.

Sharp, Elizabeth, A., Darla Johnson and Nicole Wesley. "Dance as Youth-Adult Partnership: Promoting Transformation through Reflection and Embodiment in the Teen JUSTICE Project." Eds. Francisco A. Villarreal and Yuya Kiuchi. *Youth Culture and its Influence on Communities.* New York: MacMillan ,2016. Print.

Sharp, Elizabeth, A, Schrick, Brittney, Elliot, Cara, and Huey, Cassandra (*Revise & Resubmit*). "Make sure you get at least a piece of your own cake": Stress, Perfectionism, and the Princess/Bridezilla Binary. *Journal of Marriage and Family.*

Skeggs, Beverely. "Feminist Classics Revisited" Symposium. Cambridge University, Cambridge, UK. 2013. Panel Presentation.

Smith, Dorothy E. "The Standard North American Family: SNAF as an Ideological Code." *Journal of Family Issues* 14 (1993): 50-65. Print.

Weiss, Robert. *Learning from Strangers*: *The Art and Method of Qualitative Interview Studies.* New York: The Free Press, 1995. Print.

Wink, Joan. *Critical Pedagogy: Notes from the Real World.* 4th ed. Boston: Pearson, 2011. Print.

Appendices

Appendix A: Excerpt from Pilot Survey: Lubbock Performance, August 2012

There are no right or wrong answers. We are interested in your experiences, both aspects of the concert you like and aspects of the concert you don't like and/or may not understand. Your honest responses will help improve future dance performances and collaborations between social scientists and arts faculty.

We remind you that your participation is voluntary and questions can be skipped if you feel uncomfortable answering any of the questions. No names are linked to the answers.

Background information. We'd like to understand the composition of our audience for tonight's performance.

1. Have you ever helped a plan wedding? Yes/No. If yes, how many weddings? ___ - How involved were you in the wedding planning?
2. Have you participated in a wedding? Describe your role.
3. Approximately how many single women over age 25 (including yourself) do you know well (i.e., are part of you close circle of friends and/or family)? _____ Would you say that you understand single women and their experiences? Yes/No/Not Sure. Please explain._____
4. Why did you attend the concert tonight?

Please answer the following questions after you have seen the performances. You will have 2-3 minutes between dances to write responses and more time after the entire concert.

1. What were your impressions/thoughts of the dialogue used at the beginning of the concert?
2. Would you consider the dialogue?
3. Very helpful
4. Somewhat helpful
5. Not really helpful
6. I don't really remember the dialogue
7. Other, please explain _____
8. What is your interpretation of the first dance?
9. What is your interpretation of the second dance?
10. What is your interpretation of the third dance?
11. What is your interpretation of the fourth dance?
12. Do you have a particular favorite dance or dances? Explain.
13. Were there one or more dances that you didn't like? Please explain.
14. What is your interpretation of the concert as a whole? You could describe images, themes, narrative ideas, emotions, or other responses.
15. What questions do you have?

Appendix B: Focus Group Questions, Blacksburg Performance, March 2013

Please tell us how you heard about the concert.
1. What are some of your impressions of the performance?
2. Probes: How did you make meaning from the concert, both its individual components and the larger whole?
3. Did you find the organizational structure of the concert helpful? Please explain.
4. Were there things that did not work for you, as a viewer? Please describe.
5. What did you think of the cupcakes and the factoids?
6. How was this concert similar to or different from than other dance concerts you've seen?
7. Would you have liked more information about the research that served as the framework and stimulus for the choreography? Explain.
8. Would you have liked more information about the choreography or choreographers?
9. Would you have liked more information about the researcher?
10. Any other information you would like to share? Or any other questions you might have?

Thank you for your time. Please take a few minutes and fill out a demographic sheet.

Appendix C: Text Messaging (Real Time Responses) Survey

Please send a text to XXX-XXXX before the performance starts. You will receive texts during intervals—the questions are the same as below. If you prefer not to use a cell phone and want to participate, please use this sheet to answer the following questions at the intervals.

INTERVAL 1:
What is your reaction to the dance "I Was Happy in the Pictures"? What (if any) questions does it make you ask?

INTERVAL 2:
What is your reaction to the dance "A Thin Line"? What (if any) questions does it make you ask?

INTERVAL 3 (this precedes Intermission):
What is your reaction to the dance "Dressed"? What (if any) questions does it make you ask? What are your overall impressions of the concert, including the dialogues, thus far?

INTERVAL 4:
What is your reaction to the dance "With Doubt"? What (if any) questions does it make you ask?

INTERVAL 5:
What is your reaction to the dance "The Cowboy, The Lawyer, and The Stork"? What (if any) questions does it make you ask?

INTERVAL 6:
What is your reaction to the dance "To Find My Voice"? What (if any) questions does it make you ask?
What is your reaction to "Brave" (single woman being written on)? What (if any) questions does it make you ask? What are your overall reactions to the concert, including the lobby comments, cupcakes, and napkins?

Any other comments you wish to share?

Thank you for your time!

APPENDIX D: PILOT AND FINAL CONCERT PROGRAMS

PROGRAM A: Pilot Performance: *Ordinary Wars**
August 30, 2012
Blackbox Theatre, Creative Movement Studio
Texas Tech University

Marriage Dialogue
Performers: Genevieve Durham DeCesaro, Sarah Mondle

pregnant with doubt
Choreographer: Kyla Olson
Performers: Cathey Brown, Kyla Olson, Emily Winton
Music: Sigur Rós: "Andvari"

Choreographer's Statement: In making this work, I found the dialogue from the interviews quite compelling, serving as a springboard for the movement I created. The participants had varied stances about children, from traditional to what might be viewed as less conventional. I took those viewpoints, as well as my own, and created movement to represent women who were either strongly for, against and apathetic to bearing children. Circular movement and pathways were used as themes to represent cycles in life, indecisiveness and all things maternal.

I Was Happy in the Pictures
Choreographer: Genevieve Durham DeCesaro
Performers: Ali Duffy, Kris Olson, Sarah Mondle
Music: Dakota Suite: "A Quietly Gathering Tragedy"; Peter Broderick: "We Enjoyed Life Together"

Choreographer's statement: This trio used as its stimulus six statements excerpted from the data. The statements are not connected in a linear way, but each contains particular imagery that, as the choreographer, I found striking in terms of communicative potential. The dancers contributed to creating movement motifs using the statements as prompts; parts of those motifs are all used within the frame of the larger dance. Taken as a whole, this particular work represents, abstractly, different ideas about a wedding day, none of them particularly joyful. I would suggest that this trio questions commonly publicized ideas about the way a woman "should" be on her wedding day. The statements pulled from the data used as stimuli for this work were: '*It's a lot harder than what I thought it was going to be*'; '*The yellow roses were gorgeous;*' '*So I wasn't like giddy or blissful or anything like that and I'm not sure why exactly I just wasn't*'; '*You can tell that I was happy in the pictures, you know it's not a fake smile*'; '*As soon as we were married my love for him increased greatly and I don't know why I guess*'; '*And I kinda felt like I had an identity crisis a little bit* '*(laughing).* '*I mean not really by any means but it kinda felt like I got lost in what he wanted.*'

A Thin Line
Choreographer: Ali Duffy

Performers: Genevieve Durham DeCesaro and Kyla Olson
Music: Olafur Arnalds: "Tomorrow's Song"
Choreographer's statement: Prior to reading interview transcripts, I had notions of my own about marriage and family, and I think those ideas influenced my choreography as much as the information and opinions gathered from the interview data. It seemed as if many women interviewed had similar negotiations or struggles with maintaining balance in their lives, and I have experienced that myself. This idea served as the nucleus of this duet, and I explored and expanded beyond this initial idea of losing and regaining balance to develop the work.

Dressed
Performers: Cathey Brown, Genevieve Durham DeCesaro, Ali Duffy, Kyla Olson, Emily Winton
Music: Michael Giacchino: "Married Life"
Choreographer's statement: This is a comedic dance. It is heavily influenced by the inescapable presence of a wedding dress, complete with all of the symbolism and meaning said dress embodies. The character of the bride re-presents many of the emotions discussed by the women in the interviews; I chose to highlight these by drawing attention to them using humor and exaggeration. While the quintet does poke a bit of fun (as did some of the study participants) at all of the drama of a wedding day, the choreography retains a central humanity expressed through the female dancers' care of and concern for the "bride.

Tonight's performance draws on Dr. Sharp's two social science research projects, examining women's lives and their ideas about femininity. One study focused on 18 young (aged 18-32) women's reflections on their wedding days and their first years of marriage. The other study is based on the experiences of 35 single women (aged 25-39) who did not want to marry and/or have children.

Wedding/Marriage Study**:
>The successful performance of femininity is a central feature of weddings. Participants indicated that their weddings were highly stressful, and it appeared that the cultural expectation of perfection was responsible for much of the stress. The wedding was characterized by two tensions: (a) the wedding is important but also trivialized (e.g., brides shouldn't get upset over "little things" such as hair); and (b) the wedding is the bride's day (i.e., be selfish) but it is *not* her day (don't be "Bridezilla"). Conflicting cultural messages were also evident in the role of being a wife. Transiting to being a wife was anchored in images of the traditional 1950's housewife—a few women embraced the image but many experienced tension, wanting to be a "good" wife but not sure what this means and struggling with how to be both traditional and nontraditional. For many of the participants, the experience can be summed up by one participant's description, *"*once you take the veil off, it's still work." Work is mutli-layered—it is physical labor (household tasks) as well as emotional and identity work.

Singlehood Study**:

> While women who chose to marry have a culturally accepted identity, women who chose to live their lives outside of that cultural narrative experience an especially complicated negotiation of their femininity. Single women are constantly asked to justify their identity because, in contrast to married women (whose status in viewed as permanent and stable), singlehood is viewed by society as temporary and unstable. Participants identified various reasons for not wanting marriage (i.e.., political, not a goal in life, no models for a happy marriage, feminist beliefs, "marriage is a bad business deal") and/or children ("too many children already in the world," "children would take away from my activism work"). Despite these desires, they experienced subtle and explicit pressure to marry and have children, which, in turn, prompted questioning and doubts. They were frequently told, "…you will change your mind when you are older." The passing of time created anxiety, especially about children. One woman explained that as she was aging, she felt like her "back was being pushed up against the wall." A conflict between reason and emotion characterized several participants' identity negotiation.

**For both studies, Dr. Sharp closely examined participants' words (using constructivist grounded theory) and looked for patterns across their experiences.

PROGRAM B: Pilot Performance: *Ordinary Wars**
August 30, 2012
Blackbox Theatre, Creative Movement Studio
Texas Tech University

The performance tonight draws on Dr. Sharp's two social science research projects, both examining women's relational lives and their ideas about femininity. One study focused on 18 young (aged 18-32) women's reflections of their wedding days and their first year of marriage. The other study is based on the experiences of 35 single women's (aged 25-39) who did not want to marry and/or to have children.

Marriage Dialogue
Performers: Genevieve Durham DeCesaro, Sarah Mondle

pregnant with doubt
Choreographer: Kyla Olson
Performers: Cathey Brown, Kyla Olson, Emily Winton
Music: Sigur Rós: "Andvari"

Choreographer's Statement: In making this work, I found the dialogue from the interviews quite compelling, serving as a springboard for the movement I created. The participants had varied stances about children, from traditional to what might be viewed as less conventional. I took those viewpoints, as well as my own, and created movement to represent women who were either strongly for, against and apathetic to bearing children. Circular movement and pathways were used as themes to represent cycles in life, indecisiveness and all things maternal.

I Was Happy in the Pictures
Choreographer: Genevieve Durham DeCesaro
Performers: Ali Duffy, Kris Olson, Sarah Mondle
Music: Dakota Suite: "A Quietly Gathering Tragedy"; Peter Broderick: "We Enjoyed Life Together"

Choreographer's statement: This trio used as its stimulus six statements excerpted from the data. The statements are not connected in a linear way, but each contains particular imagery that, as the choreographer, I found striking in terms of communicative potential. The dancers contributed to creating movement motifs using the statements as prompts; parts of those motifs are all used within the frame of the larger dance. Taken as a whole, this particular work represents, abstractly, different ideas about a wedding day, none of them particularly joyful. I would suggest that this trio questions commonly publicized ideas about the way a woman "should" be on her wedding day.

A Thin Line
Choreographer: Ali Duffy
Performers: Genevieve Durham DeCesaro and Kyla Olson
Music: Olafur Arnalds: "Tomorrow's Song"

Choreographer's statement: Prior to reading interview transcripts, I had notions of my own about marriage and family, and I think those ideas influenced my choreography as much as the information and opinions gathered from the interview data. It seemed as if many women interviewed had similar negotiations or struggles with maintaining balance in their lives, and I have experienced that myself. This idea served as the nucleus of this duet, and I explored and expanded beyond this initial idea of losing and regaining balance to develop the work.

Dressed
Performers: Cathey Brown, Genevieve Durham DeCesaro, Ali Duffy, Kyla Olson, Emily Winton
Music: Michael Giacchino: "Married Life"

Choreographer's statement: This is a comedic dance. It is heavily influenced by the inescapable presence of a wedding dress, complete with all of the symbolism and meaning said dress embodies. The character of the bride re-presents many of the emotions discussed by the women in the interviews; I chose to highlight these by drawing attention to them using humor and exaggeration. While the quintet does poke a bit of fun (as did some of the study participants) at all of the drama of a wedding day, the choreography retains a central humanity expressed through the female dancers' care of and concern for the "bride."

PROGRAM C: Pilot Performance: *Ordinary Wars**
August 30, 2012
Blackbox Theatre, Creative Movement Studio
Texas Tech University

The performance tonight draws on Dr. Sharp's two social science research projects, both examining women's relational lives and their ideas about femininity. One study focused on 18 young (aged 18-32) women's reflections of their wedding days and their first year of marriage. The other study is based on the experiences of 35 single women's (aged 25-39) who did not want to marry and/or to have children.

Marriage Dialogue
Performers: Genevieve Durham DeCesaro, Sarah Mondle

pregnant with doubt
Choreographer: Kyla Olson
Performers: Cathey Brown, Kyla Olson, Emily Winton
Music: Sigur Rós: "Andvari"

I Was Happy in the Pictures
Choreographer: Genevieve Durham DeCesaro
Performers: Ali Duffy, Kris Olson, Sarah Mondle
Music: Dakota Suite: "A Quietly Gathering Tragedy"; Peter Broderick: "We Enjoyed Life Together"

A Thin Line
Choreographer: Ali Duffy
Performers: Genevieve Durham DeCesaro and Kyla Olson
Music: Olafur Arnalds: "Tomorrow's Song"

Dressed
Performers: Cathey Brown, Genevieve Durham DeCesaro, Ali Duffy, Kyla Olson, Emily Winton
Music: Michael Giacchino: "Married Life"

Final Concert Program:

Ordinary Wars

A re-presentation of social science data through dance
featuring
Flatlands Dance Theatre

Text performed by Sarah Mondle

I Was Happy in the Pictures
Choreographer: Genevieve Durham DeCesaro
Performers: Ali Duffy, Sarah Mondle, Nicole Wesley

Appendices

Music: "We Enjoyed Life Together," by Peter Broderick; "A Quietly Gathering Tragedy," by Dakota Suite

A Thin Line
Choreographer: Ali Duffy
Performers: Genevieve Durham DeCesaro and Kyla Olson
Music: "Tomorrow's Song," by Olafur Arnalds

Dressed
Choreographer: Genevieve Durham DeCesaro
Performers: Cathey Brown, Ali Duffy, Genevieve Durham DeCesaro, Kyla Olson, Nicole Wesley
Music: "Married Life," by Michael Giachinno; "Wishin' and Hopin'," performed by Ani DiFranco

INTERMISSION

With Doubt
Choreographer: Kyla Olson
Performers: Cathey Brown, Kyla Olson, Nicole Wesley
Music: "Valtari," by Sigur Ros

The Cowboy, The Lawyer, and The Stork
Choreographer: Ali Duffy
Performers: Performers: Genevieve Durham DeCesaro and Kyla Olson
Music: "I Cried All the Way to the Altar," by Patsy Cline

To Find My Voice
Choreographer: Genevieve Durham DeCesaro
Performers: Cathey Brown, Ali Duffy, Genevieve Durham DeCesaro, Kyla Olson, Nicole Wesley

Brave
Performed by: Cathey Brown, Genevieve Durham DeCesaro, Ali Duffy, Sarah Mondle, Kyla Olson

---

The performance tonight draws on two social science research projects, one examining newly married women and the other examining women who have chosen to be single.

APPENDIX E: TIMELINE

We began work on this project in the summer of 2011, preparing a grant proposal to fund our initial research. We were awarded the grant (an internal, competitive grant scheme called the Creative Arts, Humanities, and Social Sciences award) in the fall of 2011. Almost immediately, we encountered an unexpected challenge when the social scientist accepted a temporary position with Durham University and moved to the UK for two years. From the fall of 2011 through the fall of 2013, the choreographer and the social scientist communicated primarily through email and Skype, as traditional face-to-face meetings were not possible.

One of our first actions was to set parameters for our project, including development of the different components. We decided, as previously noted, to use two of the social scientist's data sets and to create an evening-length theatrical concert based on the content of those data. At the choreographer's suggestion, we approached two additional, professional choreographers about assisting with the creation of the concert component and we hired a small ensemble of professional dancers to perform the choreography.

In the spring of 2012, the primary (lead) choreographer began to read the data sets. The primary choreographer also gave specific transcripts to each of the secondary choreographers for them to review. The primary choreographer, realizing that the amount of data could be overwhelming to the secondary choreographers, chose to highlight portions of the raw data that she submitted to the secondary choreographers; the highlighted section contained language specific to marriage, singlehood, or motherhood.

Throughout the spring of 2012, the primary choreographer and the social scientist discussed the development of the concert in terms of structure, thematic content, and inclusion of data. We recorded all of our discussion and have referenced it throughout our project. Near the end of the spring 2012 term and into the summer of that year, the primary choreographer completed a working draft of one dance and began work on a second. The secondary choreographers also began work on one dance each.

In August of 2012, with three dances in draft completion stage and one dance begun, the choreographer and social scientist presented a pilot performance to an invited audience. This performance, which also featured a theatrical reading of selecting data from the original interviews, was designed to provide the researchers with information about how viewers were interpreting the content of the concert. Based on the data we gathered, we made edits to the existing work and added new material. The primary and secondary choreographers used the remainder of that fall to finalize the content of the dances.

Because a significant portion of the choreography had not been created prior to the pilot performance, the choreographer and social scientist engaged in a video piloting of all new material in February of 2013. This video piloting provided us with important feedback on the content of the concert without necessitating a fully staged live pilot performance. After the video piloting, we finalized all elements of the concert, including lobby décor, intermission activities, program content, and pre/post-show speeches. We presented the concert for the first time in March of 2013 at Texas Tech University. Focus group and survey data were collected immediately following the performance. Also in March, we traveled with our ensemble of professional dancers to Virginia Tech in Blacksburg as part of a commissioned residency that included presentation of the full concert, a panel discussion, and a colloquium.

In September of 2013, we presented the concert at Texas Tech University for a second time, having been commissioned by the Board of Directors of Flatlands Dance Theatre. In February of 2014, we presented the concert and accompanying components at a commissioned residency at the University of Detroit-Mercy. We followed that presentation with an invitation from Texas Tech University's Annual Conference on the Advancement of Women to present the concert again in Lubbock in April 2015, but this time at a community theatre rather than at a theatre on a university campus. Our most recent presentation of the concert was in August 2016; we performed excerpts of the concert as an invited feature presentation at the Groves Conference on Marriage and Family in Denver.

www.ingramcontent.com/pod-product-compliance
Lightning Source LLC
Chambersburg PA
CBHW062027290426
44108CB00025B/2811